Spiritual Thirst

RAJINDER SINGH

ALSO BY RAJINDER SINGH

Spiritual Thirst

RAJINDER SINGH

SK PUBLICATIONS

© Copyright 2004 SK Publications

4 S 175 Naperville Rd., Naperville, IL 60563 USA

ISBN 0-918224-45-4

Book and cover design by Valerie Brewster, Scribe Typography

PHOTO CREDITS:
Cover photo and photos in Introduction, dedication page, and Chapters 2, 3,
    and 5: Dean Pennela Photography
Photos in Chapter 1, 4, and 6: Comstock.com
Photo of the author: Santokh Kochar

Printed in Canada by Printcrafters, Winnipeg

*This book is dedicated
to my spiritual Masters,
Sant Kirpal Singh Ji Maharaj &
Sant Darshan Singh Ji Maharaj,
who have helped quench the spiritual thirst
of millions of seekers and disciples
throughout the world.*

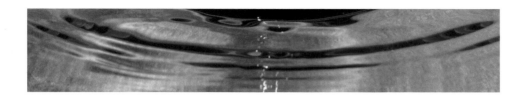

Contents

Introduction

At one time or another we develop a spiritual thirst to understand our purpose in life and the nature of our existence. Some people raise these questions but later bury them as they become caught up in the drama of their daily lives. Our quest for answers may resurface briefly during a time of pain, suffering, or loss, but is quickly forgotten as we resume our daily preoccupations. These questions will ultimately return when we face our own mortality. Some people, however, have an unquenchable thirst for spirituality and do not wait until the end of their lives to seek answers. They want answers now. They can not rest until they experience for themselves the divine nature of their soul. They seek to experience realms beyond this physical world and to discover where they came from and where they will go after this life ends.

Modern transportation and communication networks have caused the globe to become smaller, giving people all over the world instant access to detailed information from all religions and cultures. Scriptures and writings of the world's greatest saints, philosophers, and religious founders are available to all. Those with spiritual questions can learn about answers found by people in other parts of the world. A comparative study of the great spiritual writings points to one source for the answers – a source within each of us. The great religions teach that God is within us. If we wish to find spiritual answers, we need to go within our own selves.

All saints and mystics have taught spiritual practices to their disciples. These practices can be performed by any man, woman, or child of any age, religion, and culture. Whether we are well educated or uneducated in a worldly sense, or rich or poor – anyone can learn meditation.

The spiritual quest begins when we have a desire to know the answers to the mysteries of life and death. In my travels around the world I have found a growing hunger in people to learn a way to find the answers within themselves. This book is the result of fifteen years of questions asked of me by people seeking to find answers. These are the questions of people on a spiritual quest.

The questions focus on practical matters. Seekers want practical solutions. Thus, the questions go right to the heart of "What do I need to do to have spiritual realization of my self as soul and to find the higher Power?" No matter what name a person uses for that Power, whether God, Paramatma, Jehovah, Wah-e-Guru, Allah, Brahm, or Sat Purush, people want to know how to find it. Thus, the questions in this book focus on:

- how to meditate accurately

- the benefits of meditation

- inner meditation experiences

- techniques to improve meditation to increase spiritual experiences

Meditation provides a valuable tool for humanity. In the last century the world has seen tremendous growth in technological and scientific advances. We have seen innovations in transportation, communication,

medicine, and inventions to make our life more comfortable. Computer technology has made many of these innovations possible. What people are finding, though, is that all these advances do not necessarily bring them a state of peace and happiness. The scientific progress that people thought would bring inner happiness has not done so. In fact, many feel modern life has become even more stressful. With an increase in tension, people suffer from many stress-related ailments. As people seek to reduce stress and find happiness, they have been turning more to meditation. Doctors have been advising people to practice meditation to reduce stress. Researchers have been exploring the positive effect meditation has on our well-being.

With all our scientific know-how, there is still no permanent world peace. Those who are interested in a world of peace and unity realize that violence is not acceptable. There is a realization that people need to find alternative ways to bring about peace. Meditation has become accepted as a tool to help people be calm and peaceful. It provides a way to resolve conflicts. Thus, more people are trying such methods to solve problems in their personal life, in their workplace, in their neighborhood, and even in the global community.

Meditation provides a solution that can be practiced by people of all nations and all religions. It is a method that can be used by anyone, whether a believer in God, or an agnostic or atheist. People of all ages and backgrounds can learn it.

People try pursuing happiness and peace in many directions. Some have thought they could find happiness in amassing wealth, possessions, and new technological inventions, or in gaining positions of power and achieving name and fame. Yet, if we look at the lives of people who attained these, we often find they are unhappy. The things that they thought would bring them happiness did not do so. The problem with looking for happiness in anything of this world is that it is all transitory. A time may come when we lose the very thing that made us happy. Everything in this world is made of matter and as such is subject to decay. But we have within us a spiritual essence, our soul. The soul is not made of matter. Rather, it is a conscious entity made of spirit. What really brings the soul happiness is contact with the spiritual. The soul is in a state of continual ecstasy, joy, love, and Light. When we tap into our soul, we can drink from the fountainhead of this love. Those who meditate find they are filled with great peace, calm, and bliss. It is not a temporary peace, but one that is with us always. It is only a matter of turning our attention within to experience it.

The only way to reach our inner peace and bliss is to invert our attention. Right now, our attention is flowing outward into the world. Through our five senses, we are aware of the world outside and our physical body. But if we can withdraw our attention within ourselves, we will then experience the riches of our soul. The process of withdrawing our attention within has been called by different names: prayer, inversion, or meditation. If we practice a meditation that helps pull our attention to the seat of our soul, we will experience peace, love, joy, and Light. This is how inner peace can be attained.

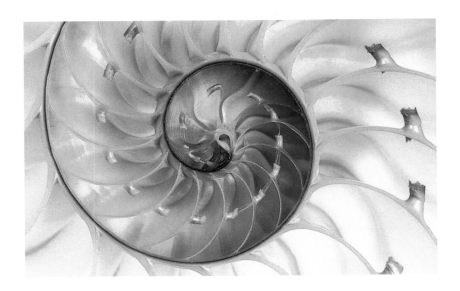

People who attain inner peace contribute to outer peace. Why? When we are peaceful, we handle outer circumstances in a much more calm and balanced manner. If we are peaceful, we will radiate that peace to those around us. If agitated, we will make others agitated. If we are happy, we can make those around us happy. When we are peaceful, we contribute to the peacefulness of others in our environment. Instead of trying to tell everyone else to be peaceful, if we are peaceful ourselves, we have contributed to the world by adding one more peaceful person to it. Rather than trying to transform others, let us transform ourselves. If each person can do this on an individual basis, then it will not be long before more people attain a peaceful state. My hope is that a day will come when the whole world will be peaceful.

It is my prayer that those filled with a spiritual thirst can have it quenched as they speed on their inner journey to spiritual enlightenment.

— Rajinder Singh

1 *Shabd Meditation*

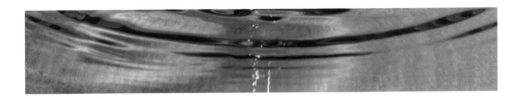

Q: What Is Shabd or Naam?

When a spiritual thirst arises within us to know our true self and know God, our search for answers begins. When we turn to the teachings of saints and founders of each religion we find similar guidelines on how to find the answers. They tell us that God is within us.

The question is: What should we do to find God within? Further research shows us that there is an inner connection between our soul and God. That connection is through what is called the Light and Sound of God, the Naam or Shabd, or the holy Word.

The beginning of our soul's journey is the contact with the Light and Sound of God, the two primary manifestations of the power of God. It is said that when God desired to bring about creation, that thought resulted in a current emanating from God. That current was manifested as Light and Sound. It was a divine stream that brought all creation into being. As it moved further from its source, the vibratory rate changed. Thus, different regions of varying vibrations were brought into being and sustain all creation. The Light and Sound principle ultimately brought the physical universe into being. Our physical universe is operating at the densest vibratory rate – so dense that it manifests as matter. It is only in the last few decades that scientists have begun to understand that what we thought was solid matter are really dancing packets of energy. At the core of matter is an energy, which is light and sound. We know that when we split an atom, there is a tremendous burst of light and sound. This light and sound energy within our physical universe is the densest vibration of the current of Light and Sound emanating from the Creator.

The Light and Sound Current flows out from God. It also flows back to God. We can catch this current at the point known as the third or single eye, or the sixth chakra. That is the connecting point between our soul (or attention in the body) and the Light and Sound Current. If we can concentrate our attention at that point, we can contact the Light and Sound Current and soar on it back through the higher regions of existence. The Light and Sound will ultimately lead us to the Source, back to the Lord.

Q: What is Shabd meditation (meditation on the Light and Sound)?

Shabd meditation or meditation on the Light and Sound consists of two practices: one is meditation on the inner Light and the other, meditation on the inner Sound. Both practices have as their ultimate goal contact with the current of Light and Sound so that the soul can rise above physical body-consciousness and travel into the inner realms Beyond.

In the practice of meditation on the inner Light, we focus our attention at the sixth chakra, while repeating the Names of God to occupy the mind, and contact the Light already within us. To do this, we begin by sitting in a comfortable position so that our body can remain still for the longest possible time. It does not require any difficult asanas or poses. Meditation can be practiced while sitting in the comfort of our own home or office, traveling in a bus, train, or airplane, or relaxing in a scenic spot of nature. It is something that can be practiced wherever we are. We may sit on a chair, on a sofa, or on the floor. We can even practice meditation lying down, but this is not recommended as it is too easy to fall asleep in this position. However, if we are ill or have a physical disability that does not permit us to sit, we can meditate lying down.

Once we select a pose, we close our eyes. That which sees the darkness is not our outer eyes; rather, it is our inner eye or eye of the soul. We then look into the middle of the field of darkness lying in front of us. When we look into the middle, our attention is actually focused horizontally, about eight to ten inches in front of us. We should not try to lift our eyeballs upward toward our forehead in the hopes of seeing something there because that puts strain on the eyes and may result in a headache. Rather, we should gaze comfortably with our eyes relaxed as we keep them before we go to sleep.

We will then find Light within. We may see Lights of various colors: red, yellow, orange, blue, green, purple, white, or golden. We may see an inner vista such as stars, sun, or moon. Whatever we see, we should continue gazing into the center. Ultimately, we will find our attention so absorbed in the inner vista that we begin to rise above body-consciousness and soar into regions Beyond.

In the meditation on the inner Sound, we listen to the Sound coming to us from within. The Sound Current will come from above and ultimately pull the soul with it on a journey into the Beyond.

In Shabd meditation, we do not have to raise our attention from the lowest chakra to the highest. Rather, we take a shortcut by beginning our concentration with the sixth or highest chakra, because it is from there that the soul leaves the body. From the sixth chakra, or third eye, we can catch the celestial Music and, like a stream, follow it back to its Source.

Q: Where does the inner journey take us?

As we are absorbed in the inner Light, we pass through the inner sky, stars, moon, and sun, and come to the gateway of the astral realm. We reach *Sahansdal Kanwal*, the capital of the astral world. This is a magnificent region, described as a thousand-petalled lotus, from which Light and Sound stream forth. The astral region has a brighter Light than this physical region and is permeated with the beautiful Music of the Sound Current that manifests as its own distinct Sound.

The soul next travels from the astral region to the causal region. The causal region has its own distinguishing Light and Sound. In this region the soul functions with a causal mind and is one with the Universal Mind. The causal region is more ethereal and its Light is brighter than that of the astral region.

Next, the soul travels to the supracausal plane. Here we find a pool of nectar, called the *Mansarovar* in which the soul bathes and sheds its causal body. The soul is now covered only with its supracausal layer. This region is beyond the mind and senses. There is absolutely no physical language that can even give us an inkling of what the supracausal realm is like. We have only pale analogies. Since the physical, astral, and causal minds have been left behind in the lower worlds, mind is of no use to us here. It is an experience of the soul. The soul experiences greater bliss and joy than in the three lower regions. The supracausal plane also has its own distinguishing Light and Sound that help the soul recognize where it is. It is in this plane that the soul, losing the forgetfulness that daunted it in the lower planes, cries out "I am That." It realizes, "I am the same essence as God."

Continuing further, the soul finally enters the purely spiritual region of *Sach Khand* or *Sat Lok* (True Region). The soul is magnetically pulled to reunite with God. The joy and ecstasy now reach an intensity beyond any human thought. Here, the region of pure Light and Sound bathes the soul. The soul is finally fulfilled.

It is with exhilaration and joyousness that the soul in Sach Khand experiences its own true state. It is in a state in which there is no pain, no sorrow, and no death. All is joyousness, love, and perpetual happiness.

Shabd Meditation has also been called *Surat Shabd Yoga*. Surat Shabd Yoga literally translates as follows: *Surat* means the soul. *Shabd* means the Sound Current, and *Yoga* means yoking or union. By uniting the soul with the Sound Current one can take the spiritual journey to the higher regions until we ultimately merge back in God.

Q: How can we learn meditation on the inner Light and Sound?

There have always been inner explorers, called Masters, who have been able to help us find the Light and Sound already within us. They teach the meditation practice on the inner Light and Sound.

They convey five Words spiritually charged with their attention to help the soul rise to the sixth chakra and into the Beyond. They also teach aspirants about pitfalls on the way. They serve as inner guides to help the soul through the numerous temptations and distractions on the inner journey to make sure that the soul reaches its ultimate goal of union with God. In every age there have been enlightened beings, mystics, and saints who can take the soul on the inner journey. They each have provided a way to keep the mind focused. The soul's treasures of love, peace, bliss, and immortality await us within. It can be fully accessed through Shabd meditation.

Q: Are there references to the Shabd or Current of Light and Sound in different religions?

There is a startling similarity to the descriptions of the Light and Sound Current given in different religious traditions. In the world's major religions, this Power is called by different names, but the descriptions are similar. The ancient Greeks referred to it as "Word" or "Logos." In the Bible it is called the Word. It says: "In the beginning was the Word, and the Word was with God, and the Word was God." (John 1:1) In Hinduism, the Word is referred to as *Nad* or *Akash Bani* (the voice coming down from the heavens), *Udgit, Jyoti* or *Sruti* (Light and Sound), or *prakash*. There are references in the Vedas and the Upanishads. In Islam, the Sufis refer to the Light and Sound Current or Word as *Sultan-ul-Azkar* (the king of prayers), *Bang-i-Ilahi, Saut-i-Sarmadi* (the Divine Song), *Nida-i-Asman* (the Heavenly Sound), *Kalam-i-Qadim* (the ancient Sound) and the Kalma or Word. In Sikhism, there are numerous references to the creative Power of the Word, called Naam or Shabd. The Zoroastrians speak of *Sraosha* or Creative Verbum.

Q: *What does the term* Sant Mat *mean?*

The words *Sant Mat* literally mean the teachings of the saints. The teachings of Sant Mat reflect the underlying spiritual truths given out by the saints who have achieved self-knowledge and God-realization. The great saints have always had love and respect for other saints and for the world's religions. They recognize that the same spiritual truths underlie each. Although outer languages, customs, way of dress, and ways of greeting others differ from region to region, the essence of religion is the same. Simply put, there is one God, we are all children of one Creator, and our purpose here is to know ourselves, know God, and have love for all.

To understand Sant Mat is to understand the basic truths underlying all faiths. Each religion has an outer or exoteric side and an inner or esoteric side. The exoteric side deals with rites, rituals, and customs related to the outer practice of religion. These often differ due to various climates and geographic features. For example, if there is an abundance of water, one may be asked to bathe before saying prayers. If one lives in the desert where it is not possible to have enough water to bathe, the custom may be to wash one's hands with sand. In some countries where it is warm, one takes off one's shoes before entering a holy place. In countries where it is cold, that may not be the custom. The esoteric or inner side of each religion is what is common to all religions. This is the side based not on theoretical knowledge, but on spiritual practices that give us a firsthand experience of our soul and God.

The basis of all spiritual teachings is God. In Sant Mat, we believe that there is one God who created all that exists. God is called by many names in various cultures, languages, and religions, but is one and the same. Whether God is referred to as the Lord, Jehovah, Wah-e-Guru, Allah, Paramatma, Ishwar, the Oversoul, Higher Power, All Consciousness, or any other names, God is eternal spirit. God is all-consciousness, all love, all Light and Sound, all peace, and all bliss.

In Sant Mat, Masters teach that God was one and wished to be many. God separated parts of Itself as souls. The soul is of the same essence as God. Thus, the soul's essence is also eternal, all-conscious, all love, all Light and Sound, all peace, and all bliss. Human beings can realize that their true essence is the soul and can realize God while in the human body. The aim of human life is to attain self-knowledge (firsthand knowledge of the soul) and God-realization. The soul resides in and enlivens the human body and can be realized through the process of inversion or meditation. In Sant Mat, the

method of meditation taught is Shabd meditation by which one comes in contact with the Light and Sound of God.

The Shabd meditation taught by the living Master at the time of initiation involves two techniques: meditation on the inner Light or *simran* practice, and meditation on the inner Sound or *bhajan* practice. The simran practice involves: stilling the body, stilling the mind through repetition of five Charged Names of God given by the living Master at the time of initiation, and withdrawing one's attention, or sensory currents, from the body and focusing it at the seat of the soul, located between and behind the two eyebrows (called the third eye, single eye, *divya chakshu, ajna chakra, daswan dwar*, or tenth door). By concentrating on the inner Light and various inner vistas described by the living Master at the time of initiation, one rises above body-consciousness and meets the inner radiant form of the Master who guides the soul on an inner journey through higher planes of creation until the soul merges back into God.

The bhajan practice involves: stilling the body and stilling the mind by listening to the inner Sound Current with which one comes in contact after initiation by a living Master. By concentrating on the inner Sound and its various manifestations as described by the living

Master at the time of initiation, one travels on the inner Sound to the higher regions until the soul merges back to God.

Within us are planes of ethereal beauty. We do not need to merely speculate about their existence, but can rise above to experience them for ourselves and know once and for all the truth that there is life after death.

Q: *Are there any benefits other than spiritual in learning Shabd meditation?*

While the main purpose of meditation in Sant Mat is purely spiritual, the practice has many beneficial by-products. Health benefits include reducing stress and stress-related ailments. Some of the intellectual benefits are improving concentration for academic goals, job efficiency, work productivity, and achievement in different fields of endeavor. Emotional benefits include developing calmness and equanimity. Its societal benefits are the achievement of inner peace and contributing to outer peace.

Sant Mat also teaches that ethical living is an indispensable foundation for spiritual progress. Ethical living includes: nonviolence, truthfulness, humility, chastity, and selfless service. In this way, while practicing meditation one can transform one's life by imbibing positive qualities.

Q: *Who can practice Shabd meditation?*

In Sant Mat, Shabd meditation is taught as a science and can be practiced by people of all religions, faiths, and belief systems. People do not need to convert or change their social or religious traditions, clothing, or customs to meditate. The meditation taught by the Masters of Sant Mat can be practiced by people of all ages, from children to centenarians, as they do not involve difficult postures or asanas, breathing techniques, or any austerities. Rather, meditation is a simple process that can be used by those who are healthy or infirm.

Q: *Does one have to leave one's home, family, religion, or culture to study Shabd meditation?*

No, Sant Mat is a path of positive mysticism in which we remain in the world, staying in our own society, culture, and family. To the best of our abilities, we fulfill our duties and responsibilities along with developing spiritually. Becoming a student of Sant Mat and learning Shabd meditation does not mean converting or changing one's religion or one's clothing or customs. One should remain in one's own religion and culture while practicing meditation. While developing spiritually, we are to lovingly and devotedly fulfill our obligations to our family, our jobs, our education and career, our community, and the world. We should help others and try to make a positive contribution to society.

Sant Mat is a practical method in which we can discover our true self as soul and rise above body-consciousness so we can reunite our soul with God. It is a way to discover our true purpose in life and reach the goal of enlightenment in this very lifetime.

Q: *Why are the spiritual teachings also called Science of Spirituality?*

Science of Spirituality is a nonprofit, nondenominational international organization that teaches Shabd meditation as a science that can be practiced by people of all countries and religious backgrounds. It also helps people to develop the ethical virtues of love, nonviolence, truthfulness, humility, and service to others. There are meditation workshops, classes, and retreats, talks on a variety of spiritual topics, and conferences focusing on meditation and spirituality. The reason it is called a science of spirituality is that meditation is practiced like a science, in which we experiment in the laboratory within ourselves. It is an organization that encourages people to try the meditation technique to see for themselves what spiritual treasures lie within. Through performing the experiment accurately, one sees for one's self the Light within and hears the Sound or inner

Music. It is only through experiencing for one's self that one can really have understanding and conviction. Reading books and listening to lectures can point the way and give the method, but the actual proof of spirituality can only come when we experience it for ourselves through meditation.

Most people think that science and spirituality are totally opposite fields of studies. I can speak from my experience in both areas that they are two sides of the same coin. To me, spirituality is the science of all sciences. The aim of science is to uncover the deepest spiritual truths, and the aim of spirituality is the search for the cause behind scientific fact.

If we look at science today, we find that one of the goals that scientists have is to discover how creation came into being and how human life began. One of the telescopes hovering above our planet is able to detect some of the earliest remains of what scientists theorize was the big Bang. By picking up signals from light-years away, we can get a glimpse of activity from the distant past whose light is only just reaching us now, billions of years later. Scientists are vying to see who can be the first to discover what happened at the moment of creation. Why? Hidden within human beings is a desire to prove the existence of a force that brought us into creation. Few are satisfied with the theory that creation was a mere accident, a combustion of cosmic dust. Secretly, in every heart, lies the desire to have proof that there is God and we are soul, a part of God. Science exists to uncover these deepest spiritual truths.

On the other hand, those engaged in spirituality are trying to find the hidden cause behind what is scientific fact. They are interested in the scientific laws of nature, but wish to go behind these laws to find the divine law that brought everything into being. While physical scientists search through outer observation and instrumentation, spiritual scientists search through inner observation by rising above this physical region of existence to higher levels of consciousness.

There are few people today who are not familiar with reports of spiritual experiences. While scriptures of all religions speak of spiritual emanations and miracles, the age of science has tried to nullify those reports as myth. However, since the 1970's and 1980's, a new wave of information has circled the planet. There are numerous accounts of people who have had near-death experiences. Although these experiences have been reported throughout history, the number of reports has increased in our time because modern science now has facility to bring someone back to life who has clinically died. Our modern medical equipment can revive a stopped heart. Thus, we find that many people who have been brought back to life report having had spiritual experiences in a world of Light while clinically dead. There are also people who have developed lower clairvoyant and psychic ability who are able to see those who have passed away and get confirmation of information imparted by the deceased that no one else could have physically known. In polls and studies, we find more people than not believe in God, the soul, and an afterlife. Such people find no contradiction between science and spirituality. They believe in scientific law as well as spiritual law.

What people take as miracles are nothing more than higher laws hidden from us. Scientists are coming to realize that this universe is not as solid as we thought. Matter is vibrating energy that appears to the physical eye as solid. When we boil the universe down to basic components we find that it is energy, Light and Sound. Performing miracles is nothing more than tapping into energy and manipulating it by the power of thought and spirit.

If we look at modern medicine, we find a whole new approach to healing. In the past we thought that healing occurred by the administration of certain drugs. A new field of medicine is exploring the mind-body connection. Researchers speak of healing the body by healing the mind and using the power of the soul. In some of the greatest medical institutions in the world, doctors are advocating meditation as a way to reduce stress and eliminate stress-related illnesses. One study revealed that people who spent time in meditation or religious worship recovered sooner from surgery than those who did not. We are living in a wondrous age in which the lines between science and spirituality are being blurred.

If you ask some of the greatest scientists how they discovered their inventions or breakthroughs, they point to a divine inspiration from a higher Power that led them to their findings. For example, Albert Einstein, who revealed the theory of relativity and made this nuclear age possible, once said, "I assert that the cosmic religious experience is the strongest and the noblest driving force behind scientific research."

When I was honored with an alumni leadership award from Illinois Institute of Technology (IIT) in Chicago, I was asked what does a scientist such as I, with my training, have to do with spirituality. I explained that science and spirituality both aim at finding truth, at discriminating between truth and falsehood.

Those who have chosen science as their field are often not much different from those who spend time engaged in the spiritual search. They are both seeking the answers to the same question, but in different ways. They both seek to know how and why reality functions.

While physical scientists gaze at the stars through powerful microscopes and listen to radio waves from distant stars through instrumentation, spiritual scientists gaze at the inner stars and listen to the inner Music of the Spheres through meditation. They both sit in silence, watching and waiting. They both search for the same answers. The physical scientists are trying to seek reality through the outer eyes and ears, while the spiritual scientists are trying to seek reality through their inner eyes and ears.

In my life I had the best of both worlds. I had scientific training from the premier institution of IIT Madras for my B.Tech. degree and IIT Chicago for my M.S. degree. I also had training from two of the greatest spiritual scientists of the last century, Sant Kirpal Singh Ji Maharaj and Sant Darshan Singh Ji Maharaj. They taught me the art of meditation and listening to and seeing the laws of the universe with the eye of the soul. I find my scientific background helped me question and study spirituality with the point of view of a scientist interested in the scientific method. In the scientific method, we test a hypothesis and carefully make observations. This scientific approach helped me prove the validity of spiritual experiences. Similarly, my spiritual background enabled me to better pursue the study of science. Meditation helps us come in touch with a level of intuition and revelation that gives us the inspiration to uncover scientific truths. As some scientists report, their discoveries came as inspiration. What is inspiration but tapping into the spiritual laws?

I feel that spirituality is the science of all sciences. Science and spirituality make a mutual partnership. If those engaged in science spend some time in the silence of their own selves, inspiration will come and lead them to the answers that they seek. Similarly, if those interested in spirituality apply the scientific law of testing hypotheses in the laboratory of their own body and soul, they will find the needed results.

I hope that those involved in scientific pursuits can discover ways to help make the world a better place as well as to find answers to the questions burning within us that drive us to uncover the greatest truths of all time – God, our soul, and the purpose of our life here.

Q: Is there a scientific explanation for the inner Music, called Naam or Shabd?

When we break down matter, we find electrons, protons, and neutrons. Science today is coming to the realization that at the heart of these smallest particles is a vibration which is going extremely fast. At the heart of matter are moving packets of energy, and the vibration given off is light and sound. For thousands of years, saints have been talking about the inner Music of God, although called by different names. It is reverberating in each particle in this universe. When our spiritual eye and spiritual ear are opened at initiation, we are able to connect with it, see it, and hear it. The Shabd, or Light and

Sound, is within each of us. As that connection is made, we rise above physical body-consciousness and soar into inner spiritual regions.

There is a definite connection between what scientists are finding out about sound and vibration and what the saints have said for many years.

Q: Why do you use the terms "empowering the soul" and "power of the soul"?

Within us, the soul's true nature is divine love, lasting peace, wisdom, fearlessness, consciousness, never-ending bliss, and eternal life. Instead of tapping into this spiritual wealth, we have empowered our mind to conceal these hidden gifts. We are ignorant of these treasures because the soul has been overpowered by its coverings of the mind, senses, and physical body. The soul has become lost in the world of mind, matter, and illusion. The soul identifies with the body and mind and has forgotten its nature. Thus, the mind and body have taken their own power over the soul. To realize our true nature, we need to empower the soul so that it can enrich our lives. Empowering the soul means that we withdraw the power that the mind and senses have on us so that our soul can instead control and guide our life.

When we empower the soul, we find ourselves filled with a love far greater than any we can know on earth, consciousness of our own self and of God, fearlessness that can help us conquer even the fear of death, immortality—for we know that even if our body dies, our soul lives forever, and eternal bliss and happiness.

2 *Fulfilling the Spiritual Thirst*

Q: *What is initiation?*

Initiation is the process of learning a meditation practice from a competent spiritual Master who gives a firsthand contact with the Light and Sound of God within. The Master conveys a portion of his life impulse or attention to the disciple to open his or her inner eye to see the Light of God and to open the inner ear to hear the inner Music or Sound of God. The Master conveys instructions for a simple method of meditation, called Shabd meditation, that helps one concentrate on the inner Light and Sound so the soul can transcend physical body-consciousness to experience inner spiritual regions of beauty, love, and Light. The meditation helps one travel on an inner current of Light and Sound through higher regions of creation until one finally attains union of the soul with God. Initiation is free and is given to all sincere seekers after truth who meet the requirements.

Q: *Who gives the initiation and what is involved in receiving initiation?*

Only the living Master can give initiation. At initiation the Master conveys initiation instructions that describe the Shabd meditation (meditation on the inner Light and Sound), gives descriptions of the inner journey, conveys five Charged Words, and opens the inner eye and ear of the disciples so they can see and hear the Light and Sound of God.

The living Master is the only one who gives the initiation and can personally convey the initiation instructions himself. The Master can also authorize a representative or group leader to read the instructions on his behalf. Even if someone receives the instructions for initiation from a representative with the living Master's approval, the initiate should consider that he or she has been initiated by the living Master. It is only the Master, and not a representative or group leader, who is giving the initiation. The representative only reads the outer instructions on behalf of the living Master, but the living Master is imparting his spiritual impulse at a spiritual level within.

Q: Is there any difference if one has the initiation instructions read by the Master in the Master's presence or if they are read by a chosen representative or group leader of the Master?

Since the initiation is a process in which the Master imparts his spiritual attention to the disciple, it is not happening at a physical level. This process takes place whether the disciple is in the physical presence of the Master or ten thousand miles away. The initiation instructions, though, are conveyed orally to the disciple at the physical level. Certain instructions regarding the meditation technique, the conveying of the five Charged Names, and the explanation of the inner spiritual journey are read out. These can be read out by the Master personally or can be conveyed by a chosen representative or group leader approved by the Master. The reading of the outer instructions can be done by anyone authorized by the Master. The inner spiritual connection to the Light and Sound that the Master gives to the disciple takes place at a spiritual level, and it does not matter whether the disciple is in the Master's physical presence at initiation or at an initiation in which the instructions are read by a representative or group leader. The charging, experience, and benefit is coming from the Master's attention and that can be enjoyed whether in the physical presence of the Master or not.

Q: *What are the benefits of initiation?*

Sant Mat teaches that by receiving initiation, which is the spiritually-charged attention of a perfect Master, a disciple will have several benefits. In this scientific age, we are taught not to believe anything unless we see it for ourselves. Numerous scriptures written by saints and founders of various religions tell us that there is God, that we are soul, and that there is more to life than this physical realm. Although reading the writings of others may inspire us, they can not satisfy us if we want the proof for ourselves. Initiation allows us to experience the truth for ourselves in the laboratory of our human body. The following are various benefits of initiation:

1) At initiation, when the Master conveys his life impulse, the inner eye and ear are opened to see and hear the inner Light and Sound of God for ourselves. That experience that he gives to start with lets seekers know that there is something beyond this physical world. The Master teaches a meditation practice that helps us transcend physical body-consciousness to experience higher inner realms. From there, we perfect the meditation practice so we can experience more and more of the inner treasures lying within waiting to be found.

2) The inner radiant form of the spiritual Master protects and guides the soul through the inner journey. The inner realms are vast. There are realms after realms within. Just as we want a guide to help us when we travel to a new country, similarly, we want the protection of a guide when we travel in the inner realms. Through initiation, the Master serves as our inner spiritual guide through the higher realms. He offers us guidance and protection as our soul journeys from the physical to the astral, causal, and supracausal regions until the soul merges back in God in the purely spiritual realm.

3) The Master gives the initiate five Charged Names that serve as a protection and password to help the soul travel through the higher planes. By repeating these Names, we are protected from any negative entity. Only a benign representative of the Positive power of God will stand before the repetition of the five Charged Names.

4) The simran practice, or repetition of the five Charged Names, helps to still the mind. One of the most common questions I receive

about meditation is: How can we still the mind so we can meditate? It seems that many people may sit for meditation, but they cannot stop the steady flow of thoughts that bombards them. When we begin to meditate we may find that our mind distracts us with thoughts. The mind is restless like mercury, always moving. In meditation, while we fix our gaze into the middle of whatever we see, thoughts may distract us. For this there is a simple remedy used by the Masters of Sant Mat. It is called simran, which keeps our inner attention focused without distraction. A spiritual Master teaches the simran practice, which consists of repetition of the five Charged Names of God repeated mentally, with the tongue of thought. These Names are spiritually charged with the attention of a Master. The charging

helps the aspirant focus the attention at the third or single eye or sixth chakra. It helps us to withdraw our attention from the world and the body below to focus at the sixth chakra. The mental or silent repetition of the five Names gives a spiritual boost to the soul so that it can withdraw from consciousness of the body, connect to the Light and Sound within, and ultimately enter a state of consciousness of the realms Beyond.

The key to exploring the inner spiritual realms and empowering our soul is to find the doorway within at the sixth chakra. The difficulty is that the mind will continually distract us from staying focused there. Thus, it is essential to learn the five Charged Words, which have the power to withdraw our attention to the sixth chakra. The five Charged Words also serve as a helpful passport as we rise from one region to the next. Thus, repetition of these Names helps unlock the doorway to each inner region.

5) The Master takes over the responsibility of winding up the karma of the disciple during his or her lifetime so the soul can achieve union with God. The Master can also adjust the disciple's karmic debts if he feels it is in the disciple's best spiritual interest, and, at times, the Master even takes on the karma of the disciple.

Sant Mat teaches that the soul undergoes a long journey through various forms of creation from the moment it is separated from God until it returns to God. This journey involves transmigration of the soul from one life form to another through 8.4 million species of life. As the soul passes through each life, it accumulates karma, a record of all its thoughts, words, and deeds. Karmas accumulated can be good or bad: good thoughts, words, and deeds; or bad thoughts, words, and deeds. Each successive life is determined by our karma. In the three lower regions of creation, the law of karma, or action and reaction, provides a system of justice in which one is rewarded for good deeds and punished for bad deeds. One must remain in the three lower regions to reap the rewards and punishments for one's karma until all karma is paid off. Since it is virtually impossible to live without engaging in thoughts, words, and deeds, one is continually accumulating karma; thus, it is nearly impossible to wind up all karmas, especially since karmas are accumulated from life to life. The only way out of the cycle is to wind up all our karmas. The trouble with doing this is that as we pay off karma, we are also making new karma. If we were to wait for the accounts to balance to zero, it could take millions of lifetimes. Thus, our soul must continue to be reborn in this physical world. The only way to escape the cycle of births and rebirths is to return to God, an eternal realm in which there is all love, consciousness, and bliss, with no pain, suffering, or death. To merge back in God and not have to return for another birth requires that our karmas be paid off. One of the great benefits of being initiated by a living Master is that the Master takes over the karmic accounts of initiates and ensures they wind it up in this very lifetime so there is no need to return for another life. In this way, they can return to the eternal bliss of union with God. The Master's commitment is to make sure that each soul taken under his wings returns to the Lord. The Master will not rest until the disciple has reached the highest realm of God and has merged back with the Source from where he or she came.

6) The Master provides outer guidance and help to the disciple in his or her spiritual progress and offers spiritual grace to the loved ones of the disciples. The living Master serves as a friend and benefactor to each disciple. The Master is there to help the disciple both in spiritual and mundane aspects of his or her life.

7) At the time of death, it is the Master who initiated us that appears to take the soul on its journey Home. The disciple will not have to meet the Angel of Death who subjects the soul to an exact accounting of all its thoughts, words, and deeds, both good and bad, committed during the soul's lifetime. The Angel of Death is there to mete out justice according to "an eye for an eye" and a "tooth for a tooth." The Master will instead meet the disciple and take care of the disciple according to the law of mercy and compassion. The Master will help the disciple to progress spiritually in the fastest possible way to make sure the soul merges back into God.

8) Once someone receives initiation from a living Master, the Master will guide the disciple until the soul attains merger back into God. The disciple may leave the Master, but the Master will never leave the disciple and will provide help for the soul's journey until it is reunited with God.

Q: *What are the requirements for initiation?*

The teachings are based on a belief that there is one God, although God can be called by any name, and we are all God's children. One requirement for initiation is that we lead a life of vegetarianism avoiding meat, fish, fowl, and eggs, both fertile and infertile, and any by-products thereof. Because we believe in nonviolence, we do not believe in killing animals to feed our bodies. Being a vegetarian means living on fruits, vegetables, grains, legumes, and milk products. Another requirement is that we should abstain from intoxicating and hallucinogenic drugs and alcohol (except if present in medication prescribed by a doctor), because they put us in a state of unconsciousness. To recognize ourselves, we need to go into higher states of consciousness. Meditation is a process that makes us more conscious,

whereas drugs and alcohol destroy our consciousness. Another requirement is that we should earn our livelihood by honest means. We believe that one needs to work for one's livelihood. We should stand on our own feet and not be dependent on anyone else unless one is a child.

Before taking initiation, one should have an understanding of the teachings through reading books and literature or through attendance at satsangs. One should also be prepared to commit oneself to meditation and leading an ethical life. We also expect people to stay in their own religions. We do not expect them to convert to anything. Basically those are the requirements for initiation. A desire and will to know God are important if we are going to be successful on the path.

We should also know that on this spiritual path it is not necessary to negate life. This path of Surat Shabd Yoga is a path of positive mysticism. We do not believe in leaving our homes, changing our customs of clothing, or leaving our place of living to permanently move to an ashram or monastery to meditate all the time. We believe that God has given us this life with a purpose. We need to fulfill our responsibilities. We believe in living in the world and discharging all our obligations to the best of our capabilities, while focusing our attention on God.

Q: Why do we need to be on the vegetarian diet and avoid alcohol and drugs in order to be accepted for initiation?

One is required to be a vegetarian and abstain from liquor and drugs to be initiated. The vegetarian diet consists of food that comes from plants or dairy products. The reason for staying away from meat, fish, fowl, and eggs is that we want to have the least destruction of life in the environment. Although vegetarian food comes mainly from plants, which are also living things, plants contain the least amount of consciousness. Eating plants involves the least destruction of the life force. On this planet, humans must eat to live. But we should eat those foods that involve the least amount of karma. Animals, birds, reptiles, and eggs all have life in them. Plants also have life, but the lowest form. They only contain the quality of water, whereas the reptiles, birds, and animals have more qualities. Since life is based on feeding the body, we stay on a vegetarian way of life, which is a cleaner way of life. We want to stay on a diet that maintains our human bodies in a way that carries the least destruction and the least karma to repay.

The reason for staying away from liquor and drugs is that we want to get into more conscious states. Meditation it is not a passive activity. It is active; we enter states of higher consciousness. Liquor and drugs are going to be slowly destroying our consciousness by putting us into unconscious states.

Thus, these are the reasons that following a vegetarian diet and abstaining from liquor and drugs are required for the way of life needed to receive initiation.

Q: Do you think someone should enter into initiation if they are not absolutely sure they can fulfill their commitments?

I do not think we should enter initiation with any doubts. We should take our time, and we should apply for initiation when we are totally sure that this is going to help us. If we have any doubts that we might not be able to make the commitments, we can take our time and get to a state where we feel totally comfortable. Only then should we decide to be initiated.

In the meantime, you can come to the satsangs. We have what we call satsangs or meetings in our centers throughout the world. Then you can seek initiation after you feel comfortable. I would never recommend to anyone to rush into initiation, because this is something that we want to do when we are totally satisfied that it is going to help us.

 Q: I understand that initiation is the mutual agreement or commitment between the Master and the student. If, during the progress of the disciple, he or she at some future time fails to meet his or her commitment to the Master, what are the consequences?

The initiation process or the commitment is not a restriction. For example, if someone was initiated and later on left the path or their commitment, there are no consequences from the point of view of any repercussions happening to him or her. But what is important to understand is that once we are connected with the divine Light and Sound of God the commitment from the Master is to guide us on our spiritual journey. This commitment helps us in many ways. According to the Sant Mat teachings, once we are initiated, if we continue with our spiritual practices regularly, then in this lifetime we can have the merger of our soul with the Creator. By the end of this lifetime, our coming and going in the world would have all ended and we would be out of the wheel of transmigration. But even if we do not follow the spiritual practices or break the commitment, then we still have the boon that we received at initiation that we will not fall below the human body. Our soul transmigrates in 8.4 million species. Once we are initiated by a perfect Master, then the greatest boon that we receive is that even though we might not be able to fulfill our commitment, we will still come back in the human form so we have another opportunity to develop spiritually. Otherwise, if we were to go through the whole cycle of 8.4 million species of life, it might be millions and millions of years before we would be able to come back into the human form.

So there are no repercussions for not fulfilling our commitments, but it does delay our spiritual progress and our return to God. It is for our own good that we fulfill the commitments.

Q: How do we experience the Master's commitment to us?

At the time of initiation, we experience the divine Light and Sound within ourselves. When we meditate and concentrate more, we go beyond the Lights, the inner sky, stars, moon, and sun, and reach our inner guide, the radiant form of the Master within, who takes us on the inner journey back to God. Then, we can receive guidance from him at all times. We get guidance in our life in many ways. The more we progress, the more we experience the Master's grace and the help we receive from him.

Q: What happens to initiates at the time of death?

Teachers of Sant Mat tell us that when we get initiated our soul is protected by the Master Power. At the time of our death, those who are not under the care of a perfect Master are met by the Angel of Death, or agents of a power referred to as Kal, responsible for sustaining the three lower regions. Kal, or the agents of Kal, will take that soul, and, based on its past karma, put it back into the cycle of lives and deaths – the wheel of transmigration. For those initiated by a perfect Master, it will be the radiant form of our Master who comes to take the soul and bring it out of that cycle of transmigration. If we have done enough meditation, if our life has been good, we can go right to Sach Khand. Sant Kirpal Singh Ji Maharaj would often say that those who live according to the teachings and meditate properly have an opportunity to go back to their true Home, Sach Khand, in this lifetime.

Some people get initiated and do not do their meditation or live according to the spiritual teachings. They walk off the path and never come back or even think about it. Yet, once the seed of initiation has been planted, that soul will not go below the human body in the next life. Once we have been initiated, then that seed has to fructify. This is why emphasis is placed on leading an ethical life and meditating for the required period of time so that, in this lifetime, we can reach our goal.

Sometimes, people may do some of the spiritual work of meditation and ethical living but not enough to return to Sach Khand in one lifetime. After death, these souls might be placed in one of the inner regions and helped there until they have progressed sufficiently to reach the goal of merger of their soul with God.

The saints have also said that God has provided a boon that time spent in meditation while living on earth in the physical region has much more effect than time spent meditating in the inner planes. That is one of the reasons they want us to meditate more and more while here in the physical region.

There are souls who, while living in the physical body, reach the radiant form of the Master and rise above physical body-consciousness and cross the physical, astral, causal, and supracausal regions to reach Sach Khand. They have gone beyond the range of Kal, the lord of the three lower regions. They experience themselves as they truly are – as soul. When they come back into the body after meditation, the silver cord, which binds a soul to the physical body during its lifetime, remains intact and is only severed at the time of physical death. These souls then can become conscious co-workers of the divine plan and help the mission of the Masters and their spiritual teachings.

Q: What is the reason that initiates are not allowed to reveal the five Charged Names to anyone else?

The great saints have said that at the time of initiation, the attention of the Master is imparted to us through these five Charged Names. These are the Names of the Power of God in each one of the five inner regions through which our soul passes. Repeating these Names, mentally, with the tongue of thought, stills the mind and helps us experience spiritual vistas within. These Charged Words also act as a testing agent so that we can test whatever appears in meditation. If we tell the five Charged Words to someone else, those words are not going to help them because there is no charging behind the words. The Masters have said that if we tell anyone the Names, then our own experiences are going to be lessened. It is a question of trust. For example, when we get initiated, one of the requirements is to be a vegetarian. If we get initiated and tomorrow say, "I am going to eat meat. What wrong can it do to me?" we are breaking our own vow. As another example, if we received the five Charged Words from the Master and were told not to reveal them to anyone, yet when the Master was in India and we were in America, we said, "What is the difference? No one is going to catch me or know or check what I am doing," then what are we doing? We are breaking our own vow. We made a pledge that we would lead a spiritual life according to the requirements explained to us. Even if we do not look at it from any other level than the practical level, we made a pledge to do something and we broke that. When we get initiated, we are told that we should keep the five Names to ourselves and not reveal them to anyone else. If we break that pledge that we took, then the help that comes to us for our spiritual growth gets lessened. That is the reason that the saints and Masters have asked us to keep the Words to ourselves and not divulge them. Someone may accidentally find out these Names; for example, if those words are mentioned in the scriptures and a person reads them without realizing what they are, they will not help the person because they lack the charging given to them by a Master. If a person does not receive them from a Master, they will not help him or her. For centuries, the tradition has been to keep the Names to ourselves. It is a sacred trust given from Master to disciple and the sanctity of this trust should be maintained.

Q: Is initiation necessary to escape the wheel of karma and attain liberation?

One of the real reasons for being initiated is to get out of the cycle of lives and deaths, or the wheel of karma. To understand this, we need to know that there are three kinds of karmas.

The first one is called sanchit karma. This is the karma that is connected with our soul that we have been accumulating from day one, when we left God's domain. Our soul has been transmigrating from one body to another. In each one of its existences, it has been collecting karma. At the end of each life, whatever karma, or whatever good and bad thoughts, words, and deeds, we have collected goes into this storehouse, which is called the sanchit karma.

Out of that storehouse, a part is taken which is called *pralabdh* karma. This pralabdh karma is also called the fate karma. An example of this is if a young person suddenly has an accident and passes away – that was already determined by their fate karma. It is also fate karma that determines that someone who is rich suddenly becomes poor, or someone who is poor suddenly finds his or her business starting to grow. Those things that we can not understand or explain logically are examples of pralabdh karma or the fate karma. These are the karmas through which we have to pass during this lifetime.

The third type of karma is *kriyaman* karma, which are the karmas that accumulate daily. Every day we have thoughts, words, and deeds. Thus, every day we are creating karma. At the end of our life, this kriyaman karma forms a part of the sanchit karma, going into the storehouse.

The process of initiation helps us escape the cycle of lives and deaths by wiping out all our karma, except the pralabdh karma. If our karma were not wiped out, we would have to come back. Even if it was good karma, we would still have to come back to reap the rewards. At the time of our initiation, the sanchit karma is wiped out through the process of initiation. It is actually the power of God, also called the Master Power, which helps us. At the time of initiation, the God Power or Master Power takes over the sanchit karma. The pralabdh karma is not touched. If the pralabdh karma were wiped out, then our existence in this lifetime would end, as we would have no more karma in this life for which we needed to keep living. Our pralabdh karmas are those that we must pass through in this current life. Whatever we are supposed to pass through according to our pralabdh karma, we pass through in this life. But those who are initiated by a living Master also receive help in passing through the

At the time of initiation our soul, covered by layers of mind, matter, and illusion, recognizes for the first time that there are divine treasures within. At the time of initiation, we are connected with the divine Light and Sound of God and start to take steps in a direction back to God.

Sant Kirpal Singh Ji Maharaj said that those who have been initiated have a great boon that if they follow the path properly, meditate regularly, inculcate ethical virtues in their lives, and lead their lives in a loving, caring, and sharing manner, then in this very life-time they can be out of the cycle of lives and deaths. Their karmas will be paid off, since their sanchit karmas were taken over by the Master Power at the time of initiation, their pralabdh karmas were passed through, and sometimes even lessened through the grace of the Master, and their kriyaman karmas were burned up through daily meditation. Thus, their karmas are wiped out so their soul can return to God when this life ends. That is the best scenario. This describes what happens to those people who follow the path properly.

For those people who get initiated and do not follow the path, their sanchit karma is wiped out anyway at the time of initiation. The pralabdh karma they have to go through. But their kriyaman karma accumulates. Since they are not meditating and are off the path, their kriyaman karma needs to be dealt with. One boon that they receive is they will not fall below the human body if they need another life. The second boon is that in their next human body they will come to the perfect Master of that time. So that is the difference between someone who has been initiated, who follows the path, who in this very lifetime can be out of the cycle of lives and deaths, and a person who has been initiated and has gone off the path, who will need another lifetime to complete his or her spiritual progress in order to be out of the cycle of lives and deaths.

Q: *What should one do if one is initiated, but one's spouse or family is not and they do not want to take initiation or they are critical of us? What is the best way to deal with the situation?*

We should never force our views on anyone. The best way to show others the benefit of the path is to live up to its teachings and become an example. If our loved ones see a positive change in us due to our taking up the spiritual path, that will cause them to take notice and see the good that has come out of the initiation. Being a positive example and being loving and caring to our family members is the best thing we can do to show them the value of the path. But if we force them, argue with them, and try to make them do something they do not want to do, they will resist. Sant Mat is a path of love. It is a path of ethical living. It is a path of caring. It is a path of selfless service. If we become living examples of the path, then it is sure to have a positive effect on our loved ones.

The best approach is to follow the principles of the path ourselves and let others live in the manner they wish to live. Each person is doing what he or she feels is best at the time. If we are loving, caring, and tolerant, we will find all our family is more likely to be accepting of us, and in due course, may also show more interest in the spiritual path for themselves.

For those who are married, it is important that we do not destroy the marriage on the basis of the path. The path should not be the basis for arguments, separation, or divorce. Rather, we should treat our partner with even more love and kindness, and show him or her that we are not interested in forcing our views or way of life on him or her. We can not give up our own commitment and principles but we should not force them on anyone else either. Through loving discussion, the spouse can be made to see that we are not going to threaten his or her way of life, and then we can live together in peace and harmony with mutual respect and tolerance.

Q: I have a few friends who have received initiation, and for one reason or another they are not putting in any effort for meditation, and I am wondering what kind of support or advice I should give them, or is it something that they have to go through?

The mind is extremely strong. Many times even when we find the right path, our mind entangles us in the activities of the world. As a friend you should not force them into anything. Number one, you can help them by being a good example yourself. Wherever there is an opportunity and they are open, you may suggest to them to meditate. If you overdo it, then people tend to feel as if they are being pushed. This path leaves it to the individual to do what makes the most sense to him or her. We can definitely tell them what is going to be good for them. As a friend, you can try to talk about the path whenever there is an opportunity. You can give them a few books to read and go from there. The saints have always said that in the Sant Mat tradition once a person has been initiated, irrespective of whatever happens to them, they are not going to fall below the human existence in their next life or lives. Even if they do not do anything to develop spiritually in this lifetime, the next time they will receive another human birth and will meet the living Master of that time. Once the seed has been put in, it will definitely fructify. We hope that it happens in this very lifetime, so they will not have to keep on coming back again. But there are some people who are not able to reach their goals in this very lifetime, so they go through more human births. Since they have been initiated, they are on the right track, and good things are going to be happening for them.

3 *Meditation Technique*

Q: What type of meditation practice do you teach?

The meditation practice is called Shabd meditation or *Surat Shabd Yoga*. It is a simple method that does not require any difficult postures, asanas, or practices. It is an easy method that can be practiced by young and old, those who are healthy and those who have health problems, as well as people of all countries and of all social, educational, religious, ethnic, or cultural backgrounds.

Q: What does the meditation on the inner Light practice of Shabd meditation involve?

To practice meditation on the inner Light – one of the two practices of Shabd meditation – we sit in a pose most convenient to us. We can sit on a chair, on the floor, or on a sofa. We can sit cross-legged, with legs straight, or in any manner. One can even meditate while standing up. For those who are physically unable to sit, they can even lie down. The reason lying down is not generally recommended is that it is conducive to falling asleep. The main thing is to meditate wherever we are comfortable. The only thing expected is that whatever pose we choose should be one in which we can sit for the longest period of time. Before the mind can be stilled, the body has to be stilled. We want to be sure that whatever pose we select, we can remain in it without moving, shaking, or scratching an itch. In whatever pose we adopt, there should be no tension in any part of the body. We should sit in a relaxed pose. Once we select the pose, we should not change it during that meditation sitting. We should remain physically still.

Once we pick a pose, we close our eyes very gently and concentrate on seeing what lies in front of us. There should be no pressure on the eyes. Our eyes should be as relaxed as they are when we go to sleep.

Since these physical eyes are not those by which we will be seeing the inner realms, there is no need to turn our eyeballs upwards in the hopes that we will see something there. If our eyeballs look or turn upward, we may feel a little pressure on the forehead, which may result in two problems. We may get a headache or we may generate heat in that area causing our forehead to become hot. That will create problems which may cause us to move or get up to do something to cool ourselves down. That will interrupt our meditation. Thus, we should not concentrate on the forehead. Instead, we should keep our eyeballs horizontal, focusing our attention a few inches in front of us, as if looking straight ahead.

When we close our eyes, we will first see darkness. That which sees the darkness is our inner eye. With the inner eye, we should gaze lovingly, sweetly, and penetratingly into whatever is in front of us. We should be relaxed but attentive, as if we were watching a movie screen and waiting for the movie to begin.

This is a process in which we do not worry about the world outside or what is going on in the body below. We are only trying to invert so as to reach the realms within. Once we close our eyes and focus our attention in front of us, the mind will try to distract our concentration with thoughts. Our mind is like mercury, always restless and moving about. We will start thinking about all our problems. We will think about the past, and we will think about the future. It could bring us thoughts about our work, families, or friends. Mind has many ways of trying to distract us from sitting in meditation and of keeping us from learning about our soul and God.

Besides our body, we have our soul and our mind. The mind is a powerful entity whose main aim is to keep our attention entangled in the physical world and our body so that the soul does not reach the inner realms. The mind will do its best to prevent us from rising above physical body-consciousness and returning to God. It will keep us constantly thinking of our problems at work or at home. The mind will engage us in continually making plans for the future. We need to realize that the soul is our real self – the part of us that is of the same essence as God. Unfortunately, we have been separated from God. If we can realize that our soul is covered by the mind and body, and understand that the mind's role is to keep us from knowing our soul, we will be better able to still our mind.

For perfect concentration, we have to reach a state where there are no thoughts. If we have any thoughts, whether good or bad, they are all bad for us as far as meditation is concerned. Thoughts are like chains. Our bad thoughts are iron chains. Although good thoughts are chains of gold, they are still chains. Thus, good thoughts are still distractions and will not help us in the meditation process.

In Shabd meditation, to keep the mind from distracting us with unwanted thoughts, five Charged Words are repeated mentally. These words are given by the Master at the time of initiation and spiritually charged with his attention. They are the Names of the Power of God on each inner region of the spiritual journey. Mental repetition of these five charged Names keeps the mind busy so that the mind does not distract our gaze with thoughts. The Names are repeated mentally, with the tongue of thought. They are repeated slowly, with a brief interval between them – not so long that it gives the mind a space to start talking to us and not so short that the Names run together.

The mind is a great distraction and keeps our attention from concentrating at the seat of the soul. However, if the mind is busy in the repetition of these Names, it cannot distract the attention with thoughts. While we gaze into the middle of what lies in front of us, we repeat the five Charged Names. The Names are to be repeated mentally, with the tongue of thought, not out loud. They are to be repeated slowly, at intervals, not in quick succession. There should be a slight pause between each Name.

While the repetition goes on mentally, we gaze at the field of darkness lying in front of us. We should not think about the world outside, the body below, or the process of withdrawal of the sensory currents from the body. We should not put any attention on our breathing. Our breathing should go on normally, just as it does when we read, study, work, or move about. As we go about our day-to-day life, we do not think about our breathing. Similarly, in meditation it should go on automatically.

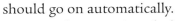

Our job is to sit calmly and quietly and lovingly gaze into the darkness lying in front of us. As we do so, the attention will automatically begin to collect at the single eye, between and behind the two eyebrows. It requires no effort. In fact, any effort we make, any thoughts we have to will ourselves to withdraw will only interfere with the process, for it means our thinking is activated. We should just go on repeating the Names of God and gazing.

There are vistas and vistas within. As the sensory currents withdraw, we forget our body. When we are fully collected at the eye-focus, we become more absorbed in the field lying in front of us. We may begin to see some flashes of Light, or Lights of various colors. We should continue to gaze with full attention into the middle of whatever is lying in front of us. Look intently and penetrate deeply to find out what is there. Our job is to look lovingly and penetratingly into whatever is in front of us and not to worry about anything else in the body. We should be totally focused on what is before us. Then, as we concentrate more and more, these Lights will stabilize and we may see red, green, blue, violet, purple, yellow, orange, white, or golden Light. Whatever we see, we should concentrate in the middle of it.

As we meditate more, as our attention is focused and we progress, we will be able to see inner vistas. We may see the inner sky, stars, moon, and sun. Ultimately, the radiant form of our spiritual Master will appear and serve as our inner guide. We will rise above body-consciousness and the radiant form of the Master will take us on the inner journey. Our soul will transcend to the astral, causal, and supracausal regions. Ultimately, the Master will take us to the purely spiritual realm, called Sach Khand, or true Realm, or true Home, where our soul merges back in God.

Through continued practice, our soul becomes adept at rising above body-consciousness, journeying through the inner realms, and returning to physical body-consciousness when our meditation time is over.

Q: Why does one concentrate on the third eye in meditation on the inner Light?

The attention is the outer expression of the soul. Most of the time we find our attention is drawn outside to the world through our senses. If we can withdraw our attention from the world outside and our body for a while and focus it at a point, known as the third eye, or the seat of the soul, we will find inner Light. The seat of the soul is located between and behind the two eyebrows. By concentrating our attention, the sensory currents that normally make us aware of sensation in our body will start to withdraw. When these sensory currents are concentrated at the seat of the soul, we can then find the Light that is already within us.

The third or single eye is the center in the body from where the soul leaves the body. Rather than beginning concentration at the lower chakras and having to work hard to raise our attention from one lower chakra to the next, Shabd meditation begins concentration at the chakra from where the soul transcends from physical body-consciousness into the inner realms beyond. In this way, it is a shorter process than beginning with the lower chakras and working our way up to the sixth chakra; in Shabd meditation, we take a shortcut by starting at the center from where the soul rises above body-consciousness.

Q: Why don't we do breathing exercises in Shabd meditation?

For this meditation process, we do not need to worry about our breathing or doing any difficult asanas or postures, or breathing exercises. We do not touch the motor currents as they do in some yogas. The motor currents are those that are responsible for the automatic or involuntary processes in the body such as breathing, circulation, the heartbeat, and the growth of hair and nails. Instead, we withdraw the sensory currents. That does not require us to worry about breathing exercises. We let the breath go on naturally as we do when we perform other functions in life. In this way, we do not have to interfere with the motor currents and the automatic, involuntary body processes during meditation.

Q: What is the second practice of Shabd meditation?

The second meditation practice of Shabd meditation is meditation on the inner Sound, or bhajan practice. The second meditation practice involves meditation on the inner Sound Current. We listen to the celestial inner Music that uplifts our soul into the realms beyond. In meditation on the inner Sound, we do not repeat the Names. We focus our attention within and hear a variety of inner Sounds. Through concentration on these inner Sounds, our soul is uplifted from physical body-consciousness to travel on the inner Sound Current into higher spiritual regions.

Q: Do you offer a meditation for those who are not initiated?

For those who are not initiated, there is an introductory technique called Jyoti meditation. The following are the instructions for practicing Jyoti meditation:

We should sit in a pose most convenient to us. We should select the position which is most comfortable, in which we can sit for the longest time. We can sit on a chair, couch, or the floor, either cross-legged or with legs straight. Those who are physically unable to sit can even lie down. Lying down is not recommended because it is too easy to fall asleep.

We should sit in a relaxed pose without any tension in the body. Once we select a pose, we should not change it during that meditation sitting. We should remain physically still.

Next, we should close our eyes very gently, as we do when going to sleep, and concentrate on seeing what lies in front of us. Our eyes should be relaxed. We should keep our eyeballs horizontal, as if looking straight ahead. At first, we may see darkness. The part of us that see that darkness is our inner eye. With the inner eye, we should gaze lovingly, sweetly, and penetratingly into whatever is in front of us. We should be relaxed but attentive, as if we were watching a movie screen and waiting for the movie to begin. Do not think about the world outside or the body below.

To provide assistance to help us bring our attention to the eye focus and to still the mind, those who have not been initiated into Shabd meditation can repeat any Name of God with which they feel comfortable. As soon as we close our eyes, the mind will try to distract us by sending thoughts. However, if the mind is busy in the repetition of a Name of God, it can not distract the attention with thoughts. While we gaze into the middle of what lies in front of us, we repeat the Name, mentally, not out loud. We repeat it slowly, at intervals, not in quick succession.

While the repetition goes on mentally, we gaze with closed eyes at the field of whatever we see lying in front of us. We should not put any attention on our breathing. Our breathing should go on normally, just as it does when we read, study, work, or move about.

We should sit calmly and quietly, while lovingly gazing within and repeating the Name of God. The attention will begin to collect at the single eye.

Through Jyoti meditation, we can experience peace, bliss, and joy.

Q: *What is the difference between Jyoti meditation and Shabd meditation?*

Jyoti meditation can be practiced by anyone. It is an introductory form of meditation that helps us get an idea of how easy meditation is. It can help us develop concentration and give us a sense of peace and calm.

For those who wish to go higher in the meditation practice, one needs to learn Shabd meditation, the technique that will open our inner eye and inner ear to see and hear the Light and Sound of God and to learn how to rise above body-consciousness to enter the spiritual realms beyond. This practice requires the help and guidance of one who has traveled the inner journey and can serve as our guide. Just as in the academic field or vocational field we want the help of an experienced teacher to train us, it is the same in the spiritual field. We want to learn from someone who is an expert in the spiritual field and has mastered the meditation technique that can take us to our goal of self-knowledge and God-realization. When we have a desire to explore the higher spiritual regions within and take the journey of our soul back to God we want to be under the guidance and protection of one who knows the pitfalls and obstacles along the way. We want someone who has been there before and can help us reach the same goal. When we want to go higher and further in our meditation, we can learn Shabd meditation from a competent Master. Shabd meditation is different from Jyoti meditation because in Shabd meditation the inner eye and ear is opened to see the Light of God and hear the Sound of God. We are given a conscious contact with the Light and Sound and are taught a method of rising above physical body-consciousness to travel on the Current of Light and Sound into the higher spiritual regions and ultimately back to our Source, God. Along with learning the techniques, the Master imparts to us his spiritual consciousness, which helps our soul withdraw to the eye focus and connect with the Light and Sound. At the time of initiation into Shabd meditation, the Master also conveys the five Charged Names that serve both as a password into the regions beyond and as a protection so that no negative power can harm us in the beyond. The five Charged Names help us steer clear of any pitfalls and distractions along the way so that we come in contact only with the positive Power of God. When one is ready to commit to the spiritual journey, one can apply for initiation into the Light and Sound, and learn the Shabd meditation.

Q: Are there any references to meditation in the different religions?

Sant Mat is based on the commonalities found in all the teachings of saints of all religions. A careful study of each religion reveals that the teachings of the saints and mystics taught the same basic truths. Among these is the need to find God within. Whether they called it prayer, meditation, inversion, or concentration, the practice and the goal is the same: tapping within ourselves to find God. Each religion or saint refers to the Light of God within and the Word of God within using different terms, such as *Naam*, *Shabd*, *Jyoti* and *Sruti*, *Naad*, *Dhun*, the Holy Word, *Kalma*, the Voice of God, *Kalam-e-qadim*, *bang-e-asmaani*, *Sraosha*, or *saut-e-sarmadi*, the Voice of Silence, or many other names. The following reference pages provide quotations from various religions and faiths on meditation and inner Light and Sound.

The light of the body is the eye: if therefore thine eye be single, thy whole body shall be full of light.

MATT. 6:22 (CHRISTIANITY)

Enter ye at the strait gate... Because strait is the gate, and narrow is the way, which leadeth unto life, and few there be that find it.

MATT. 7:13–14 (CHRISTIANITY)

And God said, Let there be light: and there was light.

GENESIS 1.3 (JUDAISM)

Thy Word is a lamp unto my feet, and a Light unto my path.

PSALM 119:105 (JUDAISM)

Meditation on Nad or the Sound Principle is the royal road to salvation.

HANSA NAAD UPANISHAD (HINDUISM)

The Voice of God comes unto my ears as any other sounds.

PROPHET MOHAMMED (ISLAM)

O God, lead me to the place from where flows the ineffable Kalma without words.

SHAH NIAZ (ISLAM)

Grow not skeptical, but attune thyself to the Sound coming down from the heavens.

MAULANA RUMI (SUFISM)

Rising above the horizon, hearken to the Melody Divine;
The Prophet would attend to It as to any other task.

MAULANA RUMI (SUFISM)

Know ye the true knowledge and meditation to be the Sound Divine.

GURU NANAK (SIKHISM)

All knowledge and meditation sprang from Dhun
     (Light and Sound principle),
But what That is, defies definition.

GURU NANAK (SIKHISM)

Every being has the Buddha nature. This is the self.

MAHAPARINIRVANA SUTRA 214 (BUDDHISM)

O nobly-born, when thy body and mind were
separating thou must have experienced a glimpse
of Pure Truth, subtle, sparkling, bright, dazzling,
glorious and radiantly awesome, in appearance like a
mirage moving across a landscape in springtime in
one continuous stream of vibrations. Be not daunted
thereby, nor terrified, nor awed. That is the radiance
of thine own true nature. Recognize it. From the midst
of that radiance, the natural sound of Reality, reverberating like a thousand thunders simultaneously
sounding, will come. That is the natural sound of
thine own real self.

TIBETAN BOOK OF THE DEAD (BARDO THODOL),
EDITED BY W.Y. EVANS-WENTZ, LONDON, 1957
(BUDDHISM)

True wisdom is different from much learning;
Much learning means little wisdom.

TAO TE CHING 81 (TAOISM)

I cause to invoke that divine Sraosha (i.e. the Word)
which is the greatest of all divine gifts for spiritual
succour.

HA 33–35, AHURAVAITA YASNA (ZOROASTRIANISM)

The aspirant is enjoined to sit in solitude and meditate
with a single-pointed attention, on the Maha Mantra
of Panch permesti and to perceive the Light.

SHRI SUTRA NANDI (JAINISM)

Finding a Time, Place, and Comfortable Position for Meditation

Q: *What is your advice about finding a good time for meditation?*

There are several things we can do to find at least two and a half hours a day to meditate. We can spend time in meditation in the morning when we awake. We might have to awake earlier than usual, but then we will be assured that we will have already devoted at least one hour to meditation before our busy day begins.

We can find the second hour in the evening. Meditation is a good way to unwind after a busy day of work. Some people like to put in one hour of meditation before dinner. Some may prefer meditating an hour before going to sleep. Others like the quiet of the middle of the night or the wee hours of the morning, when everyone else is asleep. Those who must work evening or night shift, can reverse the schedule. Then, on weekends or days off, we can easily find two to two and a half hours or more in the day to spend in meditation.

In the beginning, it is difficult to become used to a schedule. The mind tends to rebel when we try to develop a new habit. But, as it is with training in any field, after continued practice, the mind's tendency toward forming habits can be used to our advantage. With practice, the mind will become so used to meditating at a certain time that it will actually feel restless if we skip that time. When dealing with our restless mind, we need to be patient but firm. As we set up a schedule, we need to be persistent and strong in keeping to it. Over time, habit will become second nature, and we will discover that finding time to meditate will become easy, natural, and routine.

Q: I want to know about the time committed for meditation. What if I only put in a half hour a day?

As far as time is concerned, Sant Kirpal Singh Ji Maharaj would always tell us that we should donate at least ten percent of our time towards our spiritual practices, which comes to about 2.4 hours or close to two and a half hours daily. Our growth depends on how much time we are putting towards meditation.

Q: How do we balance all our daily responsibilities of work, family, and health and still find the time to put in two and a half hours of meditation every day?

We have many responsibilities in life. As a parent, we might have responsibilities to our children. As married people we have responsibilities to our spouses. As children we have responsibilities to our parents. We have responsibilities to our friends, to our work, to our neighborhood, to our country, and also global responsibilities. The great Masters are saying that these responsibilities of this world have been thrust upon us. When we are born into this physical world, our soul is given a body, and that body is born into a family. That family nurtures us. We develop love for the people in our family and become attached to them. As we get attached to them, the responsibilities of family life grow. Those attachments lead to a sense of wanting to fulfill our responsibilities to our spouses, parents, children, brothers and sisters, and friends and lead to a sense of obligation.

We should remember that we also have a spiritual responsibility. We should not forget the reason for which we have been given this human body, and that is to grow spiritually – to know ourselves and have our soul merge in God. If we forget that purpose, then all of our time is spent in fulfilling the responsibilities of this world. We may find ourselves working from morning to night, and maybe all night long. The web that Kal has created is so dense that it seems like our work never ends. It just keeps going on and on and on. The great saints say that we should recognize what is happening to us. Let us not become so engrossed in these activities that we miss this golden opportunity for truly knowing ourselves. This is why Sant Kirpal Singh Ji Maharaj as a young man early in life said when he was trying to decide what to do with the rest of his life, "God first, and everything else next." What is truly important in life is to know God, love God, be with God, and have our soul merge in God. Everything else is secondary.

Saints realize that we need to shoulder some responsibilities in our life. For this reason the path of Sant Mat is not a path of negation. This is a path of positive mysticism. We need to live in our family and in our communities, and we need to work to provide for our families. We may have other responsibilities to fulfill. On the spiritual path, we do not negate life and say, "Okay, let us leave everything and go someplace to only meditate." This path of Sant Mat is not saying that. The path of Sant Mat is saying that we need to stay in our families. We need to fulfill all our responsibilities to the best of our capabilities, but at the same time we do not forget the most important responsibility is to our soul, our true self. That responsibility is only fulfilled as we meditate. If we do not spend any time in studies, it is difficult to pass our exams; similarly, if we do not spend any time in meditation, we can not excel in the spiritual arena. We need to find the time for our spiritual practices regularly. As Sant Kirpal Singh Ji Maharaj said, "Let us give at least ten percent of our time to our spiritual practices, which is two and a half hours daily." So meditation each day is a must. We need to find time for that. Then everything else will adjust accordingly.

Sometimes we think that we do not have the time to meditate. But if we look back at our life and see the number of times that we have made adjustments to our schedule for other reasons, we would find that we could do the same for meditation. Then, everything else would fit into place. Whatever is important, we find time to do. Whatever we do not find important is left by the wayside. As we recognize the importance of this life and reaching our goal of self-knowledge and God-realization, we will definitely be able to find the time for our spiritual practices. Then, whatever other time is left over would be spent fulfilling all our other obligations.

We should make a list of priorities, putting "God first, and everything else next." In the area of "everything else next," we can list the priorities that make sense. Then we will see that everything that we consider important that we want to do will finally get done. What is interesting to know is that we struggle so much in life and say "we need to do this," or "we need to do that," and work hard for those things, but little do we realize that each of us could go at any moment. If we are writing something, it could be left off in the middle. If we have some property, that would get left behind. If we have started a new project, that would be left behind in the middle. Why? It is not important anymore. Once we are gone, who cares about those things about which we cared so much? We create for ourselves these responsibilities and say, "Oh, this is important" or "Oh, if I do not do this, this will happen." But in life, even if we are extremely busy, we can not do everything that we want to do. Things that we can not do really do not matter that much. Instead, we should give attention to what is truly important and we will find that every other aspect of our life will fall into place. As we recognize the importance of meditation, that becomes our top priority. Then, all other things will follow.

As we meditate regularly, our concentration will get better. When our concentration improves, we find that we can do a lot more in a shorter amount of time. Our clarity of thought is there. Our vision for the future is improved. Then, as we fulfill our responsibilities in the world, we feel more happiness and joy. We start to lead a life that is blissful, calm, and peaceful. That helps us to meditate better.

What is important is to recognize what is truly needed in our lives, and that is to grow spiritually and meditate. When we give that top priority we see everything else will fall into place. The twenty-four hours are going to pass, and when they are gone, whatever we did, we did. Whatever is left undone may not be that important. If we

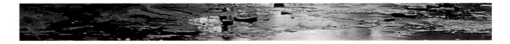

spend our time in what is most important to us and prioritize, then we will attain that which is most important. As our concentration improves through the practice of meditation we will find that we are better able to complete efficiently everything else that we think we need to do. Setting meditation as a priority is definitely helpful. The gains we achieve from spiritual progress will be more valuable than any other activities of this world.

Q: Could you speak about the importance of finding a regular place to meditate?

One of the helping factors to develop the habit of meditation is to find a special place in which to sit. Creating a sacred place in the home for meditation can help us focus our attention on meditation when we enter that area. If we reserve that place for meditation alone, then the mind will develop the habit of leaving aside all other distracting thoughts when we sit in that spot. The sacred place may be an entire room in the home, a portion of the room, or, if space is limited, a special chair or cushion on the floor. If we do not engage in any other activities in that place, then we can create an environment of peace and calm that can help us concentrate better in meditation when we sit in that area.

Q: My job has hours that shift frequently, in which some days I work day shift and some days I work night shift, or some days I travel to different cities. I can not keep a regular time and place for meditation. What should I do?

Many people in today's times have jobs that have changing hours or that require travel. In these cases, we can set up several different meditation scenarios and try to maintain regularity within the irregularity. For example, on the days that you work night shift, you can make one schedule that includes your two and a half hours meditation.

On the days that you work a different shift, you can have a different schedule. In this way, for each variation of your schedule you can still have a set schedule for meditation.

Similarly, when we travel away from home either for work, visiting family, or vacation, we can adjust our regular schedule. Just as we plan our work schedule, our time with our relatives, or our vacation activities, we can include meditation in our planning time. If we are staying at a hotel, we can always get up earlier than the time we need to get ready for work and put in time for meditation, and when we return back to the hotel room, we can put in time before dinner, after dinner, or in the evening before retiring. If we are staying with our relatives and there are a great deal of activities scheduled for us, we can make sure we get up earlier to meditate or try to meditate late at night or in the wee hours of the morning when the family is sleeping. Where there is a will there is a way.

The important point is to have some alternative meditation schedules available so that no matter what our outer situation, our spiritual practices can still take top priority.

Q: I was wondering about the time we should spend in simran and bhajan and the relationship between the two?

Simran and bhajan are the two practices of Shabd meditation that we do on the path of Sant Mat. The simran practice is to experience the divine Light and the bhajan practice is to experience the divine Sound. At the time of our holy initiation we are taught both practices and we are told that we should give ten percent of our time to our spiritual growth. Ten percent of the daily time is about two and a half hours, which would mean that half of it, one hour and fifteen minutes, is the minimum time that we are asked to give for each, and the more we can do the better. The more time we can devote, the better our chances are to grow on the spiritual path. We are asked to spend half the time to experience the divine Light within and half the time to experience the divine Sound within. Both of them lead us to rise above body-consciousness, where we experience both the Light and Sound simultaneously. This means that we may practice simran, but when we rise above body-consciousness we will be able to travel on the divine Current, which is both Light and Sound. Similarly, we may practice bhajan, but when we rise above body-consciousness, we will be traveling on the divine Current, which is both Light and Sound. So, in the practice of simran we focus on the Light, and in the practice of bhajan we focus on the Sound, but when these practices are successful and we withdraw our sensory currents we will then connect with the divine Current that is a current of Light and Sound combined.

I feel the problem or the misunderstanding of this comes in the following manner. In the East the holy Word is called the *Shabd*, another name for the divine Current, and the *Shabd* has two parts. Shabd has *Jyoti* and *Sruti*, or *Jyoti* and *Dhun*, or Light and Sound. Because the word "Shabd" in its translation is related more to Sound then to Light just by the meaning of the word in the way it is used – because Shabd also means "words that come out of you when you speak" – confusion arises as follows: the holy Word or Naam or Kalma or the Celestial Music has two components, which are the Light and the Sound. Both of these components take us to the radiant form of the Master who then guides us through the inner spiritual regions on this divine nectar or current, which is called the Shabd. Thus, our travel in the inner spiritual regions happens on this divine Nectar, composed of Light and Sound. When we do the simran practice, what we are doing is stilling our body and stilling our mind and experiencing the divine Light in front of us. So that is one means of crossing the inner sky, stars, moon, and sun and reaching the radiant form of the Master who then takes us on the journey on the divine Current to the higher planes. That is one practice that takes us there. If we do bhajan, we listen to the Sound and that also takes us to the same point. Because the literature of Sant Mat calls it the Sound Current, that is where people may have become confused. What we

call the Sound Current, or the Shabd is actually a current of both Light and Sound. I think that is where the major problem is when we read the literature because when we refer to the bhajan practice, we concentrate on Sound. When we talk about meditation on Light, we concentrate on Light. But this current, which we call the divine Nectar, is both Light and Sound, upon which we travel through the inner spiritual regions.

When we do simran, the body and mind are stilled. Simran or repetition of the five Charged Names, is a means by which we can still the mind and focus in front of us to experience the inner Light. Simran can be done at any place. You can mentally do simran if you have a lunch hour at work. You can sit at your desk and close your eyes and do simran. But bhajan is done in the privacy of your own home. Both of them are going to lead you to the radiant form of the Master who will then take you inside on the divine Nectar, which is both Light and Sound combined. That is the real vehicle on which our soul travels with the Master towards Sach Khand.

Q: Do we always do simran and bhajan in one sitting?

What we need to understand is that either one of these is the process in which we are withdrawing our attention from the world outside. As we withdraw our attention, then any distraction will bring us down to the starting point. There is the story of King Bruce and the spider. The spider goes up the wall and then falls down. Then it starts upward again, goes up the wall, falls down, goes up the wall, and falls down again. Our attention is the same way. Let us say we sit for five minutes and we have withdrawn a little bit. Then if we move or a distraction comes, our attention comes down again. Then we have to go up again from the starting point. Therefore, I would not suggest that we do five minutes of simran and then switch to five minutes of bhajan and then go back to five minutes simran, and five minutes bhajan.

That is not going to work, because then you are distracted. So I would do simran separately as long as I can, and then separately do bhajan as long as I can.

Q: *Should we do simran before bhajan, or vice versa?*

Regarding the question about whether we should do one before the other, it does not matter which one you do first. But whichever one you do, you should do it in its totality. Whether you do simran first or bhajan first, it does not matter.

Q: *How long do we do each of the two meditation practices: simran and bhajan?*

How long do we do each one? The answer is, as long as possible. The longer, the better. The example of the spider explains the reason. If our attention goes up a bit and then falls down and we have to start climbing up again, how can we reach the goal? The longer time we sit for meditation, the more chances we have of getting into deeper and deeper states of meditation. The less time we have, the less deep the states we can reach. Sant Kirpal Singh Ji Maharaj gave us two and a half hours as the minimum time that we should spend in meditation. That does not limit us. If you want to spend four, six, eight, ten, or twenty hours or whatever time you can put into meditation, so much the better. Whatever is the most time you can give, you should try to give.

I would take my two and a half hours and do one hour fifteen minutes of one and totally do one, whichever one we want to do first, and after the one hour fifteen minutes do the other one. If I only have an hour fifteen minutes at a certain time of day, then I would do one practice at that time and then I would find another one hour fifteen minutes to do the other practice at that time so we do not do both of them in one sitting. The key is not to intermingle the two practices because that would be distracting to us.

Both of these practices are vehicles by which we are actually withdrawing our sensory currents. Our sensory currents need to withdraw to the seat of the soul before we start to have the inner experiences. Any distraction is going to affect our withdrawal process to reach the radiant form of the Master and the inner spiritual regions.

Q: Should we interrupt simran to start bhajan and vice versa?

We should not interrupt one to start the other. I would not put an alarm clock and sit for meditation and say, "One hour fifteen minutes is over"—arummmmm—the alarm clock rings, and we are done. Then we say, "Golly, I am done with this thing." I do not think that is a good thing to do. Once you sit, you should let yourself go. Whenever you get up, you get up. But if you think, "I am going to meditate for one hour exactly," and then you set an alarm clock or timer, the mind is always thinking: "Twenty-nine minutes now, or is it thirty-one minutes?" Then you open your eyes to see where the clock is. That is not good to do.

Q: Do simran and bhajan ever blend into one?

Both the simran and the bhajan take us to the radiant form of the Master and on the divine Current of Light and Sound or divine Nectar, which emanates from God. In both practices, our soul rises into the inner spiritual regions. So both these two techniques do blend and take us to the same goal.

I would like to stress that the great Masters have said that we should devote as much time as we can to both of these holy meditation practices because they are the means by which we are truly able to connect with the divinity within ourselves and soar into the inner spiritual regions.

Q: It is said that we should find a quiet and calm place to start our meditations. Sometimes there is noise in the house from the activities of the family, the television, or noise from the city streets or environment outside. Can you give advice on how to meditate in a noisy environment?

We can eventually meditate in the environment in which we find ourselves. The reason a noise-free environment helps is that it makes it easier for our attention to be focused. As we learn the techniques of meditation, we can reach a state where we can meditate whether there is noise or not. If there is a great deal of noise, I would try to meditate at a time of the night when most people are sleeping. Then, as our concentration improves, we can meditate even when there is noise around. In history, we know of the story of Sir Isaac Newton who was lost in concentration as a band passed by. Later when someone asked if he heard a band pass by, he replied, "What band? Where?" He could concentrate without being disturbed by outer noise. Developing the ability to do this is a matter of being able to focus our attention. We too can perfect the ability to concentrate on our meditations even in a noisy environment and learn not to let it affect us.

Q: Could you explain the need for sitting still in meditation?

We need to keep the body still in meditation as an aid to the withdrawal process. Shabd meditation depends upon withdrawing the sensory currents from the body. There are two currents in the body: the motor currents and the sensory currents. The motor currents are those that govern automatic and involuntary bodily processes such as respiration, digestion, and growth of our hair and nails. In Shabd meditation we do not interfere with the motor currents. Instead, the process of Shabd meditation involves withdrawal of the sensory currents. The sensory currents are those that make us aware of sensation. The sensory currents are usually spread throughout the body. When we focus our attention in meditation, the sensory currents begin to withdraw from the body below and concentrate at the single or third eye, located between and behind the two eyebrows. In this way, meditation does not interfere with our breathing and those functions that keep the body going.

This process requires our body to sit still. If we begin withdrawing the sensory currents from the feet and legs to the torso, but then we move our legs, the sensory currents drop back down. Then we have to start the withdrawal process all over again. Until we perfect the technique of immediately withdrawing to the eye focus, in the beginning stages we tend to have to spend more time concentrating to reach the eye focus. Thus, if it takes us the first fifteen to thirty minutes to withdraw, then any movement in the body will bring our attention back down and we have to start the withdrawal process from scratch. If we realize that sitting still will speed up the time that we spend withdrawing our sensory currents, we will be more likely to lay stress on the importance of sitting still for longer and longer periods.

Q: *What other advice do you have for helping us to sit still in meditation?*

For a successful meditation, one of the first steps is to keep the body still. In the beginning, when we are not used to meditating, we might find this step difficult. Suddenly we want to shift position, scratch an itch, move our body around, or keep getting up. When we understand the importance of sitting still in meditation, it will help us to develop this ability. In meditation, the sensory currents need to be withdrawn from the body. When our attention is dispersed throughout the body and the senses, we are aware of our body and the sensory input coming to us from the world outside. It is only when all the sensory currents are withdrawn and our attention is focused at the third eye that we can rise above the body. Any movement will bring our sensory currents back into the limbs of the body. Then, we have to start the process of withdrawal over again. Although in meditation we are not to pay any attention to the withdrawal process, any movement brings our attention back down. If we understand this, then we will know that we will have to restart the concentration each time we move. Thus, it is important to select a comfortable and relaxed pose in which we will not have to move.

Another thing that we need to do to sit still is to remain wide awake. It is difficult to sit when we are sleepy. Our body starts to fall over or our head starts to nod and we may distract ourselves with these bodily movements. When we sit in meditation, we want to be wide awake.

Another helping factor to avoid body movements in meditation due to sleepiness is diet. Diet can have an effect on our ability to stay awake. Many people find that eating a heavy meal before meditating could make one feel sleepy. They may find that eating a light meal or keeping the stomach empty or slightly empty may keep them more awake. Sant Darshan Singh Ji Maharaj has said, "If we eat too much we feel sleepy and drowsy, and for those on the spiritual path, more time spent sleeping means less time for meditation. Even when we do meditate, if we overeat we may feel drowsy."

An important factor that will help us to sit still is to make sure we find a pose that is the most comfortable in which we can sit for the longest possible time. One of the reasons Surat Shabd Yoga or Shabd Meditation is called an "easy" yoga is that it does not ask us to sit in difficult asanas or poses required in other yogas. We do not have to contort our body or go through ascetic or torturous practices to find God. While meditation does require practice, it is relatively easier than other yogas because we can practice it in a comfortable pose. Thus, if we have physical disabilities or challenges that do not allow us to cross our legs or sit for long periods of time, we can find a pose in which we can sit comfortably. We should try different poses and select one in which we can sit for the longest time. We can use pillows and cushions to prop us up.

All these factors can help us sit in one pose for the longest possible time.

Q: Whenever I start to meditate, my body begins to itch, or I start sneezing or coughing, or some physical problem distracts me from sitting still in meditation. What should I do?

Let us analyze what is happening. Think about the time you spend sitting at a desk at your job, sitting in front of a television set or at a movie, or any other activity in which we spend time. We do not allow itching, sneezing, or coughing to stop us from doing our work, from driving, from watching television, or doing any other activity. Why do we let these distract us from meditation? We should be aware that as we try to meditate, the mind will send many types of distractions to keep us from meditating. The moment we try to sit, we feel that our head starts to itch, we have an itch on our back or legs, or we suddenly start coughing. If we were not bothered by itching or coughing before we sat for meditation, why should these start to arise the moment we close our eyes to meditate?

The first thing is to be aware that these are tricks of the mind to disturb our meditations. If we do not have a true medical condition before we sit for meditation in which we really do have a rash, or a cough, or cold, then we should be aware that these are tricks to distract us. We should try to overcome them and ignore them and keep meditating. If this is an ongoing problem, we can try to practice sitting still for a period of time each day without meditating, just to train our mind, with the goal of increasing our time to sit still. If we can only sit still for five minutes without itching, coughing, or sneezing, which are not caused by a medical condition, then we can each day increase the time by a small amount. The next day, we can practice sitting still for six minutes, seven minutes, ten minutes, and so on. Then, we can transfer our ability to sit still physically without meditating to the skill of sitting still physically in our meditations. Over time, our attention will become so focused and concentrated that we will not succumb to these distractions.

On the other hand, sometimes we really do have a physical problem. We may have a rash, insect bite, allergic reaction, cold, allergy, hay fever, or physical conditions that do make us itch, cough, and sneeze. We would be having this with or without meditation. In such a case, it is suggested that we seek advice from a medical practitioner who can help us get these under control during the time we wish to meditate so we are not disturbed. Similarly, if we have any other physical ailment that is interfering with our ability to sit still or concentrate, we can ask a medical doctor for assistance in finding a way to provide us with at least two and a half hours daily relief from our problem so the medical condition does not prevent us from meditating.

 Q: I have physical problems and can not sit up for a long period of time. I enjoy meditation and like to sit, but my body gets physical pain after a while and I have to lie down. But when I lie down, my attention is pulled down or I fall asleep. How can I meditate for a longer period of time? Should I force myself to sit up even though my body is in such pain or should I go lie down and take the risk of falling asleep? What should I do?

If your body is in pain when you sit, then you should definitely lie down or take up a position in which there will not be any pain in the body. If you have physical pain in the body when you sit for meditation in any pose, what will happen is that your attention will go to the pain. As soon as your attention goes to the pain, you are not going to be able to meditate.

You should take up a pose in which your body is relaxed and there is no pain. You should try different positions or prop yourself up with cushions or pillows. But after trying that, if the only position that truly works is lying down, then in that situation you should lie down.

The reason you fall asleep is because the body is tired. Once we lie down when the body is tired, it is conducive to falling asleep. We should try to meditate at times when the body is well rested and we are not tired. If we start to meditate at a time when we are tired, then we are going to fall asleep easily.

The other aspect of trying to relieve pain is that if we improve in our meditations, then, in whatever position we are, we are able to withdraw quickly from the physical body. We are able to rise above physical body-consciousness. As that happens, and as our attention is engrossed in whatever we are experiencing which is divine, then we will become oblivious to any pain in the body because our attention is not in the pain. Our attention is in seeing the Light of God or in hearing the Celestial Music. I would suggest that we lead our lives in a manner in which we can perfect the technique of meditation. For example, someone asked Hazur Baba Sawan Singh Ji Maharaj, "How long does it take to get to Sach Khand?" Hazur closed his eyes and opened them up and said, "I was just there and came back." Within a twinkling of an eye he could go to Sach Khand and return to physical consciousness. If we can get to that state, then if we close our eyes, we can reach the radiant form of the Master right away. Then if there is a pain here or there, it is not going to bother us because our attention would be in the divine Light and Sound of God.

My recommendation is that if you are sitting and if you have meditated for a while and then you start to find a pain in the body because sitting in that position is giving you pain, then I would take up a pose, whether it is lying down or standing up or some other pose in which there would be no pain in the body and try to meditate at that time in that pose. If the body is so tired that as you lie down you fall asleep, then I would try to meditate at a time when the body is well rested.

Q: When we are sick and can not sit up in bed to meditate, is it all right to lie down to meditate?

Although it is preferred to sit up to meditate, some physical disabilities or ailments require that we have to remain lying down. If that is the case, it is better to meditate lying down than not meditate at all. To prevent the tendency to fall asleep, if we do have to meditate lying down, we should do so when we are wide awake and have had sufficient sleep. In this way, we are more likely to stay awake while meditating lying down than drifting off to sleep.

Q: During meditation, I feel vibration in the body. What does this mean?

Sometimes when the sensory currents begin to withdraw we may get a feeling of tingling or a feeling as if we were in an elevator going quickly to the top of the Sears Tower. However, physical vibration is not a part of Shabd meditation. Shabd meditation involves withdrawing of the sensory currents from the limbs and torso until they finally reach the third or single eye. As the sensory currents withdraw from each part of the body there would be no sensation in those parts of the body. If there is a feeling of a vibration not associated with a tingling within the soul, then the vibration could be something that needs to be physically checked out with a medical doctor.

It is possible that you are confusing the spiritual experience of the soul feeling upliftment with the physical feeling of a vibration. When the soul receives a spiritual boost, or starts focusing the attention on the inner Light and Sound, the soul may be experiencing the intoxication and exhilaration of coming in contact with the God Power. It may be experienced like an effervescence or some stirring or movement, but that is not of the physical body; that is an experience of the soul. The soul is starting to feel the joy and excitement of finally being freed of its physical entanglement with the body so it can contact its own essence, the Light and Sound, the Master Power, or the Power of God. If this is what you are experiencing, then that is a natural part of the soul's stirring as it comes in contact with its Source, the God Power.

You can evaluate whether the vibration is due to some physical condition that is not associated with the meditation practice, or whether it is the tingling of withdrawal, or whether it is not actually vibration in the body, but an experience of the soul's ecstasy as it connects with the Light and Sound of God.

Q: What do I do about numbness in the legs when I meditate? When I sit in meditation, I sit in what I consider a comfortable pose. But as I try to bring my focus to the eye center, over the course of time, my legs or back become numb. Although it feels painful and I try to keep my focus at the third eye, I can not help but think about the pain. I am wondering if that is the mind playing tricks on me or is it something else? What should I do to prevent it from distracting my meditation?

What is happening is that when we sit for meditation, the sensory currents are trying to withdraw from the body. First, our feet will grow numb, then our legs become numb, and then the thighs and the middle torso become numb. The reason it might sometimes feel painful is because we are still not totally concentrated and are still focusing on the body. My suggestion to you would be to focus right in front of you, and do not think about how far you have withdrawn. It is natural to think, "I am totally withdrawn," or "To where have I withdrawn?" or "Am I doing the right thing?" This happens to many of us because we want to withdraw to the eye focus. We need to train ourselves to stop thinking about the withdrawal process. Remember, any thoughts during meditation will distract us, even thoughts about watching the meditation and withdrawal process. So, with practice, we will stay concentrated at the eye-focus and not pay attention to what is happening in the body below.

If you find that it is painful at a certain spot, then you could change the position even though you might have felt that it was the most comfortable position. Maybe something is happening to you at the physical level, and when you sit for awhile you might be having

some problems like that. I would suggest that if you are finding pain at the same spots, try to change the position in which you sit. But generally, as our sensory currents come up, we definitely get tingling feelings like pins and needles, especially in the beginning. When our sensory currents are withdrawn, it seems like the limbs are lifeless. When it feels lifeless, sometimes it starts to feel heavy. It feels as if there is a weight pulling us down. Then, if we put our attention back on the limbs from which our sensory currents have withdrawn, and the sensory currents return to those limbs, we may experience a tingling like pins and needles. The key is that as we withdraw we should not put attention on the limbs, which brings our attention back down. Instead, we should keep our attention on the eye-focus and only bring the sensory currents back down when our meditation is over. In this way, we will not experience any pain or numbness during meditation. We will remain unaware of it because we are focused at the eye-center. If we train ourselves to keep our focus at the eye-center, then we will find our sensory currents reach the seat of the soul and we will no longer be aware of the numbness in the body.

Q: Can we have a moving meditation or do we have to sit? Can we meditate while walking?

When we meditate, we have to be in a calm state. We may be sitting, standing, or lying down, but the body should be still. As the purpose of the meditation practice is to help us transcend body-consciousness, that can only happen when the body is not in motion. But there is something we can do all day long when engaged in activities that do not require any mental capabilities—if we are working with our hands, we can do simran in which we repeat God's Name so that our attention is focused on God. Thus, when we do simran while engaged in our worldly work, we are doing the portion of the meditation that keeps our attention focused at the eye-center or on God, without going to the next step of withdrawing from the body.

Doing simran throughout the day helps us to focus on God so

that when we sit for meditation later on, our attention is already on God and easily rises to the eye-focus. Just as a marathon runner prepares for the race, when we focus on God's Name by doing simran throughout the day, we are preparing ourselves for when we sit and meditate. But when we meditate doing the entire Shabd meditation practice, our body should be stilled and the mind should be stilled.

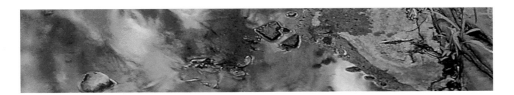

Sleepiness in Meditation

Q: I have a job and family responsibilities to my children. Then, at night, I am too sleepy to meditate. How can I still put in the minimum time of two and a half hours for meditation? How can I keep a stable meditation and not fall asleep?

It is important to recognize that we should sit for meditation when wide awake. The time that we pick to meditate should be one in which our body is well rested. Many people meditate early in the morning after they have had their sleep. In this way, when we get up in the morning, our body is rested. Many people take a shower or a bath so that they are wide awake. If we meditate at a time when wide awake, then when we close our eyes we will not fall asleep. But if we meditate at a time when we are tired or we have just come from work, chances are that when we close our eyes we will fall asleep. Please choose a time when well rested so that you do not fall asleep when you meditate.

Q: When I feel rested, and then start to meditate, it seems like the cycles of the brain are lowered or slowed down and I fall asleep. What should I do?

When we are meditating properly, we reach a state where our brain waves work between 5–8 Hz or cycles per second. Generally, while going about our daily activities, our brain waves are working at 13–20 Hz or cycles per second. If we meditate when we are sleepy, it is then that our brain waves drop to 0–4 Hz or cycles per second, which is the delta state of sleep. If we learn the proper techniques and sit when we are wide awake, then we would not fall asleep.

Q: Every time I sit in meditation, I fall asleep. I have tried doing things to stay awake, such as taking showers or reading spiritual books or stretching my body, but I still fall asleep. I also get a good night's sleep, in which I sleep for eight hours every day. What can I do?

The things that work for most people are to take a shower, sit in meditation at a time when they are not tired, or exercise. But if you are still having trouble, then my suggestion to you would be to try to meditate in the morning after you have slept for about eight hours and have taken a shower. Select times at which you are not tired.

Maybe your body needs more than eight hours of sleep. If your body needs ten hours of sleep, then you need to sleep for ten hours and then meditate. But generally, if you sleep eight hours that should be good enough.

Another factor that we need to consider is our dietary habits. Some people have a metabolism in which when they eat too much, or eat too much of certain kinds of food, their blood sugar drops and they feel sleepy. It is better to meditate on a light stomach. If we know that we are going to sit for meditation we should avoid having a heavy meal, eating too much, or eating foods that we know for a fact will make us sleepy. We should meditate when the food we eat is not going to make us tired. We may wish to consult with a medical doctor to help us regulate our diet so that we do not have a medical condition that causes us to be sleepy even if we have had eight or ten hours sleep. There are some ailments that cause tiredness, and we want to rule them out. Once we find that it is not our health or diet that is causing us to get sleepy, then we should experiment with finding a time of day when we are more awake and meditate during those times.

Try to meditate at a time when you are not tired, and with God's grace you should be able to meditate without sleeping.

Fixing the Gaze

Q: How can we fix the gaze without straining the eyes? I have trouble focusing. I have to keep on focusing my eyes. I think I am trying to concentrate too hard and straining my eyes.

In meditation, we are not trying to see anything with our physical eyes. We are gazing with the eye of the soul. Thus, there is no need to lift our eyes to our forehead in the attempt to see something there. What we see within is not with our physical eyes, but with our inner eye. What we have to do is close our eyes very gently as if we were going to sleep. Then, we should look within, just like we do at home when we are sitting across from a television set and our eyes are glued to the screen. In meditation, we should let our eyes focus about eight or ten inches in front of us. There should be no effort. Meditation on the Light and Sound is an effortless effort. When we meditate, we should not think that we need to see this or see that. When we meditate, we should pray to God to show us and give us whatever God thinks is best for us. We should sit lovingly as if we were an empty cup that is open so God can pour divine nectar into us. We do not have to make any effort. It is an effortless effort, where we sit relaxed. We close our eyes very gently and see whatever we experience with our inner eye. As we do it more and more, we will find it will be easy to do. The first few times, we might want to open our eyes or scratch here or there. These are normal things that happen to many people in the beginning. Since our body and mind do not want us to concentrate, they are trying to distract us in one manner or another. As we meditate more, then we will be able to concentrate and sit still for a longer period without any forces to distract us. We will grow accustomed to keeping our eyes focused ahead of us into the middle of whatever appears. We will no longer have to strain. We will merely watch as if a movie screen were in front of us and we were waiting for the movie to start. This will keep us from straining our eyes.

When we sit down to meditate, we should make sure that our eyeballs are straight. Some people raise their eyeballs in the hope of getting to the seat of the soul, but doing so can end up in a headache. Instead, we should keep our eyeballs straight, in a vertical plane. As we keep our eyeballs straight, our focus will become better.

One good practical exercise to increase our ability to keep our eyeballs straight might be to take a chair and put it five or ten feet from the wall and, at your eye level, put a round spot on the wall. Then, look at it for five minutes or so. Then, close your eyes and see if your eyeballs can stay at the same level all the time. That will help keep our eyes straight as we close our eyes. We will see that our concentration in meditation will automatically increase. It is a question of concentration. We need to remember that this is just an exercise for increasing ability to keep the eyes straight—it is not part of the meditation and is not required. It is just an idea we can try to keep our eyes straight ahead without looking up at the forehead during meditation time.

Q: This is a question about the meditation technique. When I meditate, after a while, I get in a relaxed state and sometimes start to drift off. Then my attention will flicker back and I will drift off again. Which is the concentration point at which I should be aiming? Is it at the place to where I have drifted off or is it at the eye focus?

We should bring our attention back into the eye focus and keep our gaze in front of us, because when we drift off, we will find that we have drifted off into some thought patterns. We do not want to drift into thought patterns. We want our attention to be at the seat of the soul, at the eye focus. This is why in Shabd meditation the repetition of the five Holy Names of God is important or, in the case of Jyoti mediation, we repeat any Name of God. We have to still our mind. When our mind repeats these Names of God, the mind is engaged in doing something and it is easy for us to focus. Our drifting happens when we are not concentrated at the third eye, and our attention has gone into another direction. We want to bring it back as soon as we can. We want to keep our gaze focused into the middle of what is lying in front of us, at a distance of about eight to ten inches in front of us.

Q: The Masters of Sant Mat tell us not to concentrate on our breathing when doing meditation on the Light and Sound. Why don't we engage in breathing practices or exercises, such as Hatha Yoga, while meditating on the Light and Sound? Will we not make the same progress in meditation on the Light and Sound when we practice Hatha Yoga, or exercises in which we concentrate on the breathing?

The practice of Surat Shabd Yoga or Shabd Meditation is to connect our spirit with the Light and Sound of God. We are supposed to withdraw our sensory currents from the world outside and collect them at the seat of the soul. We are supposed to leave our motor currents alone. The motor currents are those currents in the body through which our physical body operates. The motor currents control the breathing system, the circulation of blood, the digestive system, and the growing of our nails and hair, all of which are needed to keep our physical body alive. In the teachings of Sant Mat,  the meditative practice is to withdraw the sensory currents. Therefore, the breathing is to go on normally, just like our breathing goes on normally when we do our work all day. We do not focus our attention on how the next breath is coming. We do not focus our attention on how the heart is beating or how the blood is circulating in our system. That just keeps on happening. When we meditate, our attention should be kept in the same manner — not focusing on our breathing.

Regarding Hatha Yoga, I think what is important to understand is why people do Hatha Yoga. If you are doing the Hatha Yoga exercises because you want a spiritual experience and use the breathing exercises with Surat Shabd Yoga, then it is not going to help you progress in Shabd meditation. At the time of our initiation we are told very clearly that when we practice Surat Shabd Yoga, we are not to mix any other technique with it. So, if you take the breathing techniques out of Hatha Yoga and you mix them with the techniques of Shabd meditation of withdrawing the sensory currents, then your progress will be hampered. But if you are doing the Hatha Yoga for physical fitness and exercise for the physical body to keep the body fit and fine, and do it separately from Surat Shabd Yoga, then there is no harm in doing it. We know that the physical body also needs to be kept fit and fine. We merely need to understand that we are doing Hatha Yoga for the fitness of the body, and we are doing Shabd meditation for the purpose of connecting our soul with the Light and Sound of God to soar above body-consciousness and travel back to God.

What we need to understand is that we all have a certain amount of time in our day that we can give to ourselves. Our time is spent in getting dressed, bathing, eating, going to work, resting and sleeping. Most of our time goes there. We may be left with just a few hours that we can use in whatever direction we want. Keeping the physical body fit is fine. Whether we do aerobic exercises, Hatha Yoga, other physical exercise, or play sports, they are good because they keep the physical body in good shape. If Hatha Yoga is practiced for that purpose, then it is okay. But we should also understand that we have limited time for ourselves. So if it is recommended to do physical exercises for an hour for your system, then that is fine. But if we have four or five hours and spend all of them in physical exercise, we have no time left for any other activity. So we have to hit a happy balance in our own system.

Saints have always said that what will truly help us is meditation, which is an exercise to help the spirit. Shabd meditation helps us connect with the divine Light and Sound of God within. The spirit is nourished and receives help. We get into the best shape we can spiritually when we meditate and go within. Thus, if the Hatha Yoga practice is done for physical benefits for our body, then it is fine. But please do not use it thinking it is a vehicle to speed our spiritual progress and intermingle the breathing exercises with the techniques of Shabd meditation, because if you do, you will not get the results from this form of meditation.

It is like when we do an experiment. Suppose we are in the laboratory in school and have to do a physics or chemistry experiment. If we do the experiment exactly the right way, we get the prescribed results. Similarly, when we meditate on the Light and Sound of God, we need to do it properly, according to the method laid out and not mix in any other process or system into that practice. When we do the meditation exactly as prescribed, then we will get the desired results which will be good for our spiritual progress.

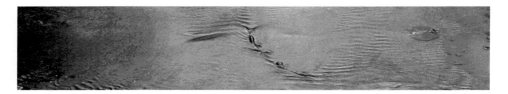

Keeping the Mind Still

Q: *How can we keep the mind still during meditation?*

The mind is in continuous motion. The harder we try to keep the mind still, the more thoughts it sends to us. The mind is like mercury; it is always restless and always moving. It can jump from images and thoughts of New York, to London, to Delhi, and back again. Those who practice meditation have grappled with this problem throughout the ages. Masters have found a solution which involves occupying the mind with a task to keep it busy: repetition of the Lord's Name. Repetition keeps the mind occupied so that our attention can focus its gaze on the field of vision lying in front of us.

The most efficient way is to repeat the Names of God mentally. This process is called simran. The concept behind the mental repetition is to keep both the body and mind still. If the tongue is moving, the attention will be on the tongue. Thus, through oral repetition our body would not remain completely still. Using the tongue also means that the sound of the Names will be audible, which will activate our attention to the sense of hearing. Mental repetition, however, does not involve any organs or senses. The mouth is still, and the sense of hearing is not activated. In mental repetition, only thought is occupied, which is precisely the point – to keep it busy. One repeats the Names of God, thus stilling the mind. While the mind is quiet, our attention can then focus at the third eye without disturbance.

In the introductory meditation instructions, Jyoti meditation, we can keep the mind occupied by repeating any Name of God that we love. Those who have received initiation into Shabd meditation are given five Charged Names to repeat, so they use that to keep the mind still. The repetition of the five Charged Names is called the simran practice. While you close your eyes, go on repeating any Name of God mentally, or if initiated, the five Charged Names. The Name or Names should not be repeated so quickly that each repetition runs into each other, nor should it be repeated so slowly that there is too much space between each repetition, giving the mind a chance to send thoughts.

Through this repetition, the mind can be kept busy so the gaze is not disturbed by extraneous thoughts. This will help still the mind for our concentration to be fixed into the middle of whatever lies in front of us. In this way, we can stay focused on the Light within and the soul can withdraw into the Light for its journey into the realms beyond.

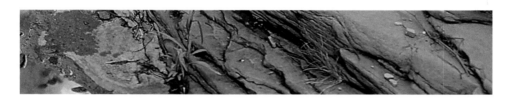

Simran and Bhajan Practices

Q: How is it possible to keep simran going on throughout the day when we are not sitting in meditation and still continue doing other activities? How can we do both at the same time?

The saints have always said that whenever we are doing an activity that is not requiring intellectual thought, such as driving the car or doing something with the hands, we should be doing simran. For those whose attention on God is strong, they can do simran while doing many different activities. We have heard about saints who meditated with their eyes open. It seems like it is not possible to meditate when your eyes are open because there are many distractions attracting our sense of sight. But once our attention is focused, nothing distracts us and we are able to do simran with many activities going on. When we are beginning to learn the simran practice, we should start with one thing at a time. We should do simran with one other activity, such as doing something with our hands. When we master that we can try doing simran with another activity, such as walking or exercising. It takes practice and concentration. Through practice, we can become proficient.

Q: What should we do if we are doing simran, but the Sound starts to come in; or we are doing bhajan, but we start seeing Light within?

When we meditate, we use two different techniques of meditation: meditation on the inner Light or simran practice, and meditation on the inner Sound or bhajan practice to hear the sweet symphonies of the Sound of God. When we do the Sound or bhajan practice, we may hear many different types of Sounds, which can include small bells, a big bell, the conch or shell, thunder, drums, veena, bagpipes, flutes, and other Sounds within ourselves. These Sounds that we hear or the Lights that we see in the beginning are all reflections of the Sounds and the Lights of the inner regions.

If we are doing the bhajan practice and hear the Sound Current, we should keep our attention on the Sound. We should not do simran while listening to the Sound Current. Simran, or the repetition of the five Holy Names of God, is done when we are doing meditation on the Light of God. If, while doing bhajan, we see Light we should not pay attention to the Light, but keep focusing on the Sound we hear coming from the right side.

When we do the bhajan exercise to hear the Sound we do not repeat simran because the Sound Current will grab our attention automatically and lift our soul up. When we do bhajan, we should not go after the Sound. We should listen to the Sound that comes to us from the right side. It actually is coming from above, but since we are used to hearing from the right side or the left side, to us it seems like the Sound is coming from the right side. That Sound is going to lift us up. We should keep our attention focused on the Sound, which will automatically raise us up.

Also, if we are doing bhajan and start seeing the Light, we should not pay attention to the Light. Rather, we should continue to concentrate on the Sound Current that we hear.

If we are doing simran, and start hearing the Sound Current, we should not listen to the Sound but stay focused on the Light.

We also should not break our meditation and switch from one to another if Light comes in during bhajan, or Sound comes in during simran. We should stick with one practice for the length of time allotted to it. We should focus on the Sound during bhajan, and on the Light during simran. In this way, we can perfect both practices by staying concentrated on the one we started to do. But we should spend time in both practices each day.

Q: I was having a problem with hearing Sound coming from both sides when I meditate in the bhajan practice, and I was trying to figure out how to eliminate this.

It seems that you are listening in stereo! You seem to be listening as a musician would, to music that comes in from both sides, but that is not what we should do in the bhajan practice. When we sit for bhajan, our eyes are relaxed, just as in simran, but we are not looking at anything. We are merely sitting in a relaxed state and waiting to hear the Sound. The Sound in the beginning will seem like it is coming from the right side. Our tendency is to take our attention and put it on the right side. As soon as we do that, the Sound starts to get less and less. Actually the Sound is not coming from the right side. It is coming from above. Because we are used to listening to outer sound through our ears in day-to-day activities, it seems like it is coming from the right ear. But if we keep our attention on the Sound that comes to us without following it to the right, it will come nearer to us. We will find that it is coming from the middle or above and will help our soul reach higher states of consciousness.

You are asking about why the Sound seems to be coming from the left? We need to recognize that as we connect with the divinity within ourselves our mind gets annoyed. Mind has its home in the third region and is a part of, or an agent of, the sustaining power, which has been known as Kal. Kal has jurisdiction over the lower three regions. It does not want us to get out of its jurisdiction. The lower three regions, which are the physical, the astral, and the causal regions, which in the East are called *Pind*, *And*, and *Brahmand*, are under the jurisdiction of Kal. Kal wants its three lower regions to

be populated. For example, suppose there is a super-king – a king who has a large kingdom. He has to manage many things. So what does he do? He has some assistants and says, "Go and take care of this area." To another assistant he says, "You go and you take care of this area." He directs a third assistant to take care of another area. When the king gives all the powers to an assistant to take care of an area, that person wants to grow his or her area; he or she does not want his or her area to be depleted. If this person's area gets depleted, his or her power becomes less and less and less. For example, in a company, the vice-president of marketing wants a larger force than the manufacturing person has. The manufacturing person wants to have a bigger force than the administrative person has. The administrative person maybe wants a bigger area than the research and development people's area. Everyone wants his or her empire to grow larger and larger. People know that if their empire gets depleted, the head of the company might say, "Oh, we don't need him or her. Just cancel his whole department. Close it down."

Similarly, Kal has jurisdiction over these lower three regions. For whatever reason, God gave Kal these souls to inhabit these regions. Kal worries that if any one of the souls gets out from these three lower regions, that is one soul less. Kal is nervous that these three lower regions will become depleted. So Kal tries hard to keep souls entangled in these lower regions.

What Kal does is that as we try to meditate, Kal starts to bring problems to us realizing, "Hey, this soul is having its connection with the Lord. As soon as the connection becomes stronger, this person is not going to be here in my region." For example, in the story about the Pied Piper he blew an instrument and everyone followed; similarly, as we get connected to the inner Light and Sound of God – our soul can follow that Current, like the Pied Piper, back to the Source. Thus, Kal can not keep that soul within its domain. So Kal wants to nip it in the bud. Kal knows that the more our connection grows, the more the experience will be more fulfilling than anything that Kal can offer in its domain and the happier we will be. The soul's desire for more and more of the bliss from the Sound Current will intensify. We will want more and more of it. Thus, Kal, right in the beginning, creates all kinds of problems so we do not pay attention to the Sound Current. Due to the difficulties created by Kal, we say, "Meditation is difficult. We can not sit. There are so many thoughts. I want to listen to the Sound from the right, but it comes from the left and is troublesome. Forget it." This is why Kal puts so many problems in front of us. One of them is to send Sounds that will pull us down, so that we can not rise above. We try to listen to the Sound coming from the right, so Kal sends a Sound from the left to confuse us. We say, "Should we listen here, or should we listen there?" It is just like when we are trying to tune into a radio station and another station booms in. That is how they jam the first station. When they want to have listening wars to get more people tuned into them, stations may jam the frequencies. That is what Kal is trying to do. So we need to deal with it.

I would suggest the following things. Although simran is not part of the bhajan practice, by improving our simran practice we will lessen the mind's hold on us. Another thing we can do is that before we go to sleep every day, for fifteen to twenty minutes, just repeat the five Charged Names, separately from everything else that you do all day and apart from your regular meditation sittings. We should repeat the simran for fifteen or twenty minutes extra over everything else that we do in our daily meditations. The next day, we will find that this will improve both of our meditation practices — meditation on the inner Light and meditation on the inner Sound, by increasing our power of concentration.

By understanding what Kal is trying to do, we will be more aware of Kal's trick in trying to send Sound through the left side and will not fall into that trap.

Even though we are trying to listen to the Sound, our focus needs to be perfect. The stronger our focus, the better we will be tuned into the divine Power within. We can use our increased concentration ability to stay focused on the right side Sound.

Q: If we do simran throughout the day while not in meditation, does that mean that we are putting in more time for simran than bhajan?

The time we spend in the meditation practice for simran and for bhajan should be about half and half. When we refer to doing simran throughout the day while doing other activities, it is not recorded as time spent in the simran meditation practice. We only record time spent in the actual meditation practice in which we sit still, close our eyes, keep our gaze focused in front of us, and repeat simran mentally.

Simran during the day is an activity that helps us in our meditation because it focuses us on God all day long. We can do that part of the simran practice in which we repeat the Names mentally while involved in other activities of the world.

If we do simran when we are not engaged in a mental activity, but while performing some physical activity, then our attention will be focused on God more easily when we sit for meditation, for either the Light or the Sound practices.

Q: Can we hear the Sound Current when not doing bhajan?

Yes, many times we do hear the divine Sound Current even when not doing the bhajan practice. When we are walking around, or when we get up in the morning, depending on the state or development of our soul, we might hear the Sound Current. If some inner Sound is coming during the day when we are not in the bhajan practice, let it continue. It is not going to distract you.

Q: If I am doing simran and I hear the inner Sound, what should I do?

There are times when we sit for simran that we hear the divine Sound Current. Why? The Sound Current is going on all the time within us. But we should not pay attention to the Sound during the simran practice. If the Sound comes during the simran or Light practice, do not focus on it; rather, keep your attention on the Light during the meditation on the Light.

Q: If we are doing simran and hear or are bothered by outer sounds, should we stop to close off our ears, such as putting on headphones or using ear plugs, so we can block out the sounds and not hear anything?

If we are doing the simran practice and start hearing outer sounds, we should not stop meditating to change our pose to cut off the outer sounds because that will distract our concentration. We should practice staying focused on simran and gazing within at the inner Light and learn to tune out outer sounds. As we become more absorbed within we will no longer notice sounds around us.

Q: What is the reason for the way of sitting in the bhajan practice?

The reason we do the bhajan practice in the prescribed way is to cut off the outside sounds so we can concentrate on the inner Sound. Generally, wherever we are, there is some outer sound which is always going on. For example, there might be air conditioners running, the sound of wind blowing, crickets chirping, or some other kind of sounds in our outer environment. It is difficult to be somewhere without any outer sounds. To develop concentration on the inner Sound, we have to be totally without any outer sound. The purpose of cutting off all outer sound is so that it does not become a distraction. The key is to get to a state of calm and quietness so that there are no sounds to create distractions. Once we reach a state of quietness, our sensory currents collect at the seat of the soul, and we become engrossed in what we are experiencing within. When focused within, the way we cut off outer sounds is superfluous. The methods to cut off outer sounds are there only in the beginning stages to help us concentrate better. When we are developed, we are able to distinguish the inner Sound from the outer sounds and can stay concentrated on the inner.

In history there were souls who had evolved and they could hear the Sound Current at all times without closing off the outer sounds. Such people could close their eyes and experience the Sound without any special pose.

It is the same thing with the eyes during the simran practice. Why do we close our eyes when we sit to experience the Light? It is so that the distractions from the outside, which are coming in through the eyes through the retina to our brain, are cut off. There are many examples of those who could have inner experiences with their eyes open. There is an example from the life of Sant Darshan Singh Ji Maharaj. Once, his Master, Hazur Baba Sawan Singh Ji Maharaj, gave him a darshan for a split second as he was leaving the ashram. Sant Darshan Singh Ji said that from that one glance of grace the form of Hazur stayed with him for days even with his eyes open, from the time he awoke, continuing throughout the day while walking, studying, and going to school. Wherever he went, his Master's form was always with him with his eyes open. Therefore, it is a question of our concentration and our attention being focused.

The purpose of closing the eyes when we sit to meditate on the divine Light is so that the outer sights do not distract us. The closing of the ears when we sit to experience the divine Sound is there because we do not want to be distracted by the sounds from the outside. So my suggestion is that if we sit for Sound, we should do the prescribed pose to cut off the outside sound and listen to the inner Sound. If we are doing simran, we should close our eyes to cut out the outer Light and try to focus on the inner Light.

 Q: I live in a noisy place, and do not know if the sound I hear is coming from within or from outside. How can I tell the difference?

This is one of the main reasons that we ask people to block out the sound during the bhajan practice so we can focus on the Sound coming from within. By blocking out the outside noise, we can be sure that the Sound we hear is coming from within.

4 Benefits of Meditation

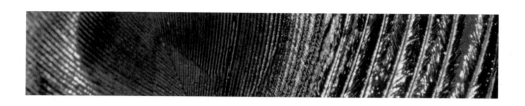

Q: *What are some of the health benefits of meditation, and how can we heal our body through meditation?*

While meditating to experience inner peace and bliss, we also get some by-products from the process. Meditation can provide us with physical benefits. Medical researchers have been exploring the body-mind connection. They have linked certain illnesses to our state of mind and emotional condition. They have found that when we undergo mental stress, emotional pain, or depression, our physical resistance to disease drops. We become more susceptible to contracting a disease because our ability to keep our immune system in top working order decreases. Science has pinpointed certain diseases such as heart disease, digestive problems, circulation and breathing problems, and migraine headaches, to name a few, to be sometimes stress-related.

Spending regular, accurate time in meditation has been shown to reduce stress. One meditation study, by Dr. John L. Craven published in the Canadian *Journal of Psychiatry*, states: "Controlled studies have found consistent reductions in anxiety in meditators... Several stress-related conditions have demonstrated improvement during clinical trials of meditation including: hypertension, insomnia, asthma, chronic pain, cardiac tachyarrhythmias, and phobic anxiety." (Craven, Dr. John L., "Meditation and Psychotherapy," Canadian *Journal of Psychiatry*, Vol. 34, October 1989, pp. 648-53).

In another study, Dr. Ilan Kutz states: "As the ability to meditate develops, a hierarchy of sensation develops, ranging from deep relaxation to marked emotional and cognitive alterations... Many of these peripheral changes are compatible with decreased arousal of the sympathetic nervous system... The peripheral physiological changes have proven to be of value as a primary or adjunctive treatment for a variety of medical disorders such as hypertension and cardiac arrhythmias, as well as in relieving anxiety states and pain." (Kutz, MD, Ilan, *et al.*, "Meditation and Psychotherapy," *American Journal of Psychiatry*, Vol. 142, January 1985, pp. 1–8).

Many medical centers and hospitals now offer classes in meditation as a way to reduce stress and eliminate certain illnesses. In this way, meditation can help us heal our physical body by healing our mind and our emotional state.

Another benefit is that by becoming absorbed within, we can divert our attention so that we do not feel the pinching effects of illness. We come in contact with a stream of bliss and joy that takes our attention away from the pains of the world. We can enter a refuge of bliss and peace within, safe from the ravages of physical pain. Another study in the United States recently reported that those who meditate and pray, and those who attend a spiritual gathering at least once a week, showed increased recovery time from surgery and illness when compared with those who do not.

Meditation helps slow down the brain waves to a state of calm. Researchers have tested brain waves and found that while we are going about our workaday life, driving in traffic, or experiencing stress on our job, our brain waves are in the beta state of 13–20 Hz or more. When we are in a creative state of learning, it goes to the alpha state of about 9–12 Hz. When we are in a state of calm, it is in the theta state of 5–8 Hz. In the theta state our mind is calm, our heart beat slows down, and the body is more relaxed. Deep sleep is the delta state of 1–4 Hz. Through meditation, we are bringing our mind and body into a state of relaxation. This can reduce the opportunity for our body to be in the state that can cause stress-related ailments. Medical researchers have reported that meditation can reduce the risks of some diseases aggravated by stress such as heart disease, digestive problems, breathing problems, headaches, and other ailments.

When the body is relaxed, the mind can begin to relax. When the mind is relaxed, the body is calmer and stress is reduced. Meditation contributes to both mental and physical relaxation.

Q: How can we heal our mind through meditation?

In this hectic world, our mind is often agitated by stress and pressures. Life has become so complicated that people seem to have too much to do and not enough time to do it. Some people hold jobs that require long hours and much responsibility. Other people work two jobs and raise a family. Too much pressure often causes people to snap – they become irritable, off-balance, and stressed-out. They begin to act in ways that are not themselves. Sometimes they take out their frustrations on their loved ones and hurt those they should love the most.

Meditation is a way to eliminate the lack of balance caused by our mental stresses. By spending time in meditation, we create a haven in which we restore equilibrium to our mental functioning. Through meditation our mind becomes calm and our stress levels will be reduced.

Besides reducing stress during meditation, there is a carry-over effect. We will find that we can maintain our peace of mind as we continue our activities throughout the day. As we perfect our meditations, we can maintain that calm state of mind even in the midst of turmoil and strife. We will find ourselves in control of our reactions and we will maintain an even keel in the face of other people's conflicts.

Another benefit of meditation is the change in our angle of vision. As we rise above body-consciousness, we find there is more to our existence than what goes on in the physical world. We see the larger picture and realize the higher values of life. We have read about those who had near-death experiences who reported the importance of being loving and helping to others. The petty trifles of life no longer bothered them because they realized that when they leave the world nothing else matters except having been loving and giving. Meditation gives us that same angle of vision. Thus, we do not become embroiled in all the petty trifles of life but stay focused on our higher goals.

Through meditation, we can bring about a healing of our mental state and can, over time, develop the equilibrium of mind to function more effectively and more peacefully in this world.

Q: How can we heal emotional pain through meditation?

Family life has changed dramatically. In many families in which both parents have to work, people have less time for their children. Young people are often raised by baby-sitters, childcare centers, and daycare centers. With the breakdown of extended families, or with people moving to places with better job opportunities from areas where their own immediate relatives live, children no longer have easy access to grandparents, aunts, and uncles to care for them when their parents work. Sometimes, even if one moves in with one's extended family, there is tension between different family members. Children, in increasing numbers, are not receiving the kind of love and attention they need to become whole, emotionally healthy people.

There is also an increase in abusive marital relationships, drug and alcohol addictions, child abuse, and dysfunctional families. With an overemphasis in society on academic achievement and career preparation, we have not devoted enough time in our western society to learning how to get along with others, establish good human relationships, develop parenting skills or relationship skills for a healthy marriage, and cope with emotional pain. The result is an increase in the number of people who have emotional problems. What used to be considered a problem of only a few, now has become a problem of the masses – psychological and emotional pain.

Psychologists often identify these pains as remnants from an unfulfilled childhood. The popular phrase for curing this condition in the West is called "healing your inner child." This refers to the feelings we had as a child that were never healed. We may have been hurt and abused by our parents; or we may have felt unloved, uncared for, abandoned, rejected, and shamed. When the important adults in a child's life do not help the child resolve these pains, the person carries these wounds into adulthood. Their emotional growth is stunted at a childhood level. Although these people grow up and have an adult body and adult mental capacity, their emotions may be still functioning at a childhood level. Thus, when other adults hurt them, criticize them, reject them, or do not act loving towards them, adults with that inner-child pain react as they did when they were children:

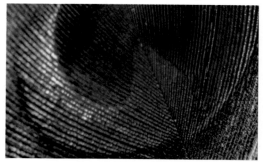

they cry, act out, run away, withdraw, throw a tantrum, and act childishly among other adults. The pain of crisis reopens their childhood wounds and they play out the same pain over again in adulthood. Each time they are wounded, more scarring is added to the wound. Instead of healing, the wound becomes more traumatized, and people become so hypersensitive that they can no longer cope with adult situations. They may begin to avoid people, build defenses, or act aggressively even in minor conflict situations.

Meditation can supplement the various forms of therapy that people use to heal emotional pain. As people work on their emotional problems, often with the guidance of trained specialists, they can increase their healing by meditating.

Meditation helps emotional pain in several ways. First, by rising above the body we can see our lives from a clearer angle of vision. We begin to recognize the roots of our pains and can start to solve the problems. Many people are not even aware of why they act and feel the way they do. By raising our consciousness we become aware of the causes of some of our feelings. We can then pinpoint the area of our life in which we need to work. In meditation, we come in contact with the source of all love. The current of Light and Sound is made of the same essence as our soul and the Oversoul. That essence is love, consciousness, and bliss. As we come in contact with it, we experience divine love. We connect with the love of God latent within us. It is said, "God is love, the soul is love, and the way back to God is through love." We may not have had love as a child and may still be suffering from those wounds, but contact with godly love fills that hole with more love than we can ever imagine. We can get an idea of that love by reading about the near-death experiences that people had. They describe coming into the presence of a being of light, who radiated more love to them than they ever felt in their entire lives. In fact, the love was so profound and fulfilling, many did not want to return to their bodies – and this is just describing near-death experiences that merely touched the border of the higher regions. The love found in the higher regions is even greater than that which is described in near-death experiences. Those saints and religious founders who traveled through meditation to higher regions than the ones encountered through near-death experiences have described in their writings the overwhelming love they experienced beyond. St. Catherine of Sienna speaks of it as a mystic marriage with God. Mystics and saints from India speak of union with God as an eternal marriage with their Beloved. Being drenched in that love fills the void in the heart left over from childhood pains. Thus, meditation can be an effective process for healing emotional pains.

Q: How can we heal the soul through meditation?

Our soul is already healed. Our soul is already whole. We just need to connect with it. It is our disconnectedness that causes spiritual pain.

Even more poignant than the pain of the physical body, the mind, and the emotions, is spiritual pain. The hunger for God causes a pain deeper than any other kind of anguish. St. John of the Cross refers to it as the "dark night of the soul." We want to see our Maker, we want to know the ultimate Truth, and we want to unravel the mystery of our existence, yet we do not find the answers. Sant Kirpal Singh Ji Maharaj once said, "Once the question of the mystery of life and death enters our heart, we can not rest until we find the answer." In fact, he himself when beginning his spiritual search in his youth would shed tears day and night for God to lead him to someone who could provide the answers to these mysteries.

When spiritual thirst grips us, we begin our search. This is our spiritual awakening. We may search for the answers in our religions. We may read the scriptures, attend our places of worship, and perform rites and rituals. If we do not find the answer there, we may explore other religions and faiths. If we do not find the answer there, we may take up a form of yoga, or spiritual discipline. Ultimately, when we analyze the path walked by those who found the answers – saints, mystics, religious founders, and spiritual Masters – we come to the same conclusion – the way lies within, and we can reach it through meditation.

Shabd meditation can uplift our soul to realms in which we can find the answers to all our spiritual questions. We can journey, while still alive, to the regions that await us when we ultimately leave our physical body at the time of death. The burning question, "where do we go after we die," will be answered because we will have already journeyed there in life through meditation. Death will no longer fill us with fear, for we will see for ourselves that it takes us into the beyond where there is more bliss, joy, and love than we can ever imagine.

We will see ourselves as soul, as a Light of God, and know that we are drops of the Oversoul. Ultimately, we will reach the stage of merger with God and become all-conscious. It is at that stage of unification that our spiritual thirst is quenched. We no longer yearn for love – we become love itself.

Q: *How can we heal the world through meditation?*

As each person heals his or her pain and becomes whole through meditation, other phenomena take place. Each person becomes an instrument in bringing about a healing of the planet. When we become peaceful within ourselves, when our physical, mental, emotional, and spiritual pains are healed, we radiate that peace to others. We are no longer a source of conflict, but become a remedy for conflict. We no longer hurt others in thought, word, or deed. Instead, we apply balm to others' wounds.

When we rise above this world through Shabd meditation, we see the Light of God in all and love all creation as one family of God. We become an agent of peace and goodwill, an ambassador of love. If each person offered their soothing presence to those with whom he or she came in contact, it would not be long before we would heal the world of the scars of war, of hatred, and of inhumane acts. Outer peace would be assured and a golden age of spirituality would begin.

Q: What can medical doctors do to help heal their patients through Jyoti meditation?

As researchers document the physical benefits of meditation in reducing stress-related ailments and decreasing the healing time of those recovering from illness or surgery, they find that meditation serves as another tool in the doctor's medical bag to offer patients. While providing medical care and treatment to patients, doctors can also advise their patients to spend time in meditation as a preventative health care measure and a supplement to medical treatment.

There is an introductory form of meditation, Jyoti meditation, that can be done by anyone. It can be practiced by anyone of any religion, culture, or age. It is a process that can be practiced by young children as well as those over one hundred years of age. It does not involve any difficult asanas or practices. It is a safe process that involves withdrawal of our sensory currents.

To practice Jyoti meditation, we can sit in a pose that is most convenient in which we can remain still for the longest possible time. Doctors who have patients who cannot sit up can recommend to them to meditate lying down. We close our eyes gently and focus our attention on the field of darkness lying in front of us. By concentrating, the sensory currents begin to withdraw to the single eye. When concentrated there, we find peace within. We can sit on a chair, on the floor, or on a sofa, either cross-legged or with legs straight. We can sit in any manner.

Once we close our eyes and focus our attention in front of us, the mind has many ways of trying to distract us from sitting in meditation and of keeping us from learning about our soul and God. In Jyoti meditation we can repeat any Name of God with which we feel comfortable. If the mind is busy in the repetition, it cannot distract the attention with thoughts. While we gaze into the middle of what lies in front of us, we repeat any Name of God. The Name is to be repeated mentally, with the tongue of thought, not out loud. It is to be repeated slowly, at intervals, not in quick succession.

While the repetition goes on mentally, we gaze at whatever we see within lying in front of us. We should not think about the world outside, the body below, or the process of withdrawal of the sensory currents from the body. We should not put any attention on our breathing. Our breathing should go on normally, just as it does when we read, study, work, or move about.

Look intently and penetrate deeply to find out what is within. Whatever we see within we should concentrate in the middle. Through Jyoti meditation, we can experience inner peace and calm.

The solution for all our pains and the world's pains is available to every human being on this planet. By spending some time daily in meditation, we will be in continual contact with a healing power that can transform our lives and give us relief and solace.

Q: Can meditation help one improve productivity on the job, and how?

Yes. Meditation increases our ability to concentrate. This increase in concentration affects other aspects of our life. Students are better able to concentrate on their studies. Many students who meditate have told me of improvements in their test scores. We also have better concentration on our jobs. We can focus longer and are more productive and efficient. Some places of work provide a one-hour meditation time for all employees before they begin their work day and they have done measurements to show how their employees' productivity increased. The increased concentration and relaxation that we receive through meditation can help us deal with time pressure, stress on the job, and multiple tasks in a calmer, easier, and more efficient way.

Q: *What are some other benefits of meditation?*

Being in a state of calm, peace, and happiness has an effect on many other aspects of our life. One area in which we will find improvements is in our personal relationships. Our family life with spouses, children, and parents can improve because we are dealing with situations in a more balanced manner. For those who are dealing with issues of feeling unloved or uncared for due to an unhappy childhood, meditation can help us tap into a source of love within that will not leave us. By filling ourselves up with the love and happiness of our soul, we may find relief from many of the emotional scars and pains of life.

We may find an improvement in our interpersonal relations with other people on our jobs or in our social lives. As we meditate, we begin to see life from a higher angle of vision. When we tap into the peace within, it flows out from us to others. They are affected and we will find they may also deal with us in a better way.

5 *Inner Experiences*

Q: If we start meditating and see swirling colors does that mean we are on the higher planes?

When we first close our eyes, we begin to see different flashes of Lights, colored Lights, or swirling colors. If we are seeing these before we have reached the radiant form of the Master, then we are seeing only reflections of the Light of the inner regions. To reach the higher planes we first need to pass through the inner sky, stars, moon, and sun, and reach the radiant form of the Master who will take us to the higher planes. Until that happens, any swirling colors, flashes of Light, or different colored Lights that we see in meditation are only reflections of the Light of the higher regions. We need to go beyond that. Even though we get joy and bliss in seeing the Lights, this is just a first step. We have to go beyond the colored Lights to the inner sky, stars, sun, moon, and meet the radiant form of our inner guide. Only then does our inner spiritual journey start.

Q: Do the inner experiences of colored Lights, sky, stars, moon, and sun, and the radiant form of the Master always come in the same order when we meditate?

We may see any one of these when we close our eyes to meditate. On a particular day, our attention may be so withdrawn that when we close our eyes we immediately see the radiant form of the Master. On another day, we may begin with the inner moon or sun. Although the order in which one passes through these stages is the same, sometimes we start out seeing one rather than another. The key is, whether we first see the inner sky, the inner moon, or merely different colored Lights, we have to get to the radiant form of the Master to take the inner journey. On different days we may have different inner experiences. For example, we may begin with the radiant form of the Master and then lose concentration so that our attention goes to darkness or colored Lights. Then, we have to bring our attention back to the Master's form. Although the order of the inner journey is the same, what we see during a meditation sitting may differ each time.

 Q: Sometimes when I begin to withdraw quickly from the body and start to rise above body-consciousness I feel afraid and it pulls me back down into physical body-consciousness. What should I do?

The first time or first few times the soul begins to rise above body-consciousness, some people are not used to it so they feel afraid and that fear pulls their attention back down into the body. We need to know there is nothing to fear. Fear arises for two reasons. One is fear that we will not return to the body. We should know that there is a silver cord that connects the soul to the physical body. That cord remains intact when we meditate. It is only severed when our number of breaths is used up and it is time to pass on. Meditation does not interfere with the silver cord and it remains connected throughout the meditation practice. So we should not fear rising above the body. We are not going to die; we are merely peeping inside to experience the beautiful realms beyond. When the experience is over, we are still in the body.

The second thing that may scare us is that we think we are actually leaving the body. The term "rising above body-consciousness" is a misnomer. We are not actually going out of the body into the sky or space of this physical world. We are actually shifting our consciousness between two concurrent states that co-exist simultaneously. It is like when we are watching television and we shift our attention from watching the screen to experiencing hunger in our stomach or a pain in the legs. We can shift our attention from any part of the body, to looking at something with our eyes, to thinking about something in our mind, to remembering something that happened to us in the past, and back again to a pain in our arm. Similarly, we are not really rising above anything – we are merely shifting our attention from  this physical realm to the inner realms. Because the sensory currents are withdrawing from our legs to our torso to our third eye, it may feel as if we are rising. But even though we enter the eye-focus, experience the inner sights, meet the radiant form of the Master, and travel into the realm beyond, we are not rising above the body. We are merely shifting our attention to these inner sights. If we understand this, the fear of rising out of the body will subside because we will know that we are shifting our attention to a different state of consciousness without affecting our physical body.

The other reason we may experience fear is due to the mind and Kal trying to distract us from our inner progress. It is not our soul that is in fear; it is the mind that becomes fearful. The mind is an agent of Kal, who wants us to remain in the three lower regions. Kal fears that a soul may escape from its domain. When Kal finds us progressing to the point that we are rising out of the body to travel on the inner Light and Sound Current to the higher planes, it panics. That panic is reflected into its agent, our mind, who fears that its end is near. Mind knows that its home is up to the third region. The soul's home is in the fifth region beyond. If the soul progresses, the mind worries about its end. The mind wants to keep control over the soul. We should recognize what the fear is but not succumb to it; otherwise we are giving in to Kal and its agent – the mind. We should move past the initial fear and let go to soar within. We are merely going on an elevator ride to a higher region. When that journey is over, we will return to body-consciousness. We should recognize what the fear is and tell ourselves, "Keep going. This is our chance to soar within to experience unspeakable bliss, love, and permanent happiness." We should go with the exhilarating experience and enter the beyond. Once we get past the fear and soar on this inner journey, we will not experience the fear anymore.

Q: What if we hear a voice in our meditation?

If a voice from within tells us to do something, we must not listen to that voice but ask the form to appear before us, and then test it with simran. Simran is a testing agent so that if Kal is trying to distract us, we can repeat the five Charged Words or simran to test whatever power is there. If it is not a positive Power that can help us to reach Sach Khand, that negative entity will go away and will not distract us. Only if the form comes forward and remains before the repetition of simran should we listen to the voice.

Q: Why should we keep our spiritual experiences to ourselves?

There are several reasons to explain why we are asked not to reveal our inner experiences to others, except to the Master. First, we live in a world in which there is a lot of competition. Everyone wants to do and be better than the other person. When we are in this competitive mode, each one wants to become better and better. In that process, there is a risk that one can become egotistic. In meditation, the experiences of each of us are going to be different. While we are all on the same path back to God, our awakening and our growth on the spiritual path are different. When we talk to others about our inner experiences, what happens is that those whose experiences are not as good as ours become jealous of us. That creates tension, friction, and problems between them and us. Therefore, the Masters have suggested that we keep the experiences to ourselves, because those experiences are between our soul, the Master guiding our inner journey, and God. That is a reason that we have been asked to keep the experiences we have within to ourselves.

This spiritual path is not a path of boasting or of being egotistical. This is a path in which we want to be humble. If we look at the lives of the great saints and mystics, they all called themselves servants of God. If you look at how Hazur Baba Sawan Singh Ji Maharaj, Sant Kirpal Singh Ji Maharaj, or Sant Darshan Singh Ji Maharaj wrote, they went even further – they called themselves "the servant of the servant of God." They considered their own Master as the servant of God, and they were then the servant of God's servant. We also need to inculcate that virtue of humility along with truthfulness, nonviolence, chastity, and selfless service. Humility is an important aspect of our life. We need to be humble. We need to lead a life in which we have love for all and do not feel as if we are above anyone else, whether it is other human beings, animals, insects, or any other living form. That aspect of humility is important.

Sant Darshan Singh Ji Maharaj would say in his satsangs that ninety-nine point nine recurring percent of humility is found in the saints. When you look at a true saint, you will find that they are extremely humble. When we look at the life of Sant Kirpal Singh Ji Maharaj or Sant Darshan Singh Ji Maharaj, we find how humble they were and how lovingly they met everyone. Whether someone was unkempt, unwashed, or sweating, when someone came to Sant Darshan Singh Ji, he would always embrace them, irrespective of who came to him. It was a love within him that poured out to us. It was due to his humility that he would greet others lovingly, irrespective of their caste, color, creed, or whatever status of life they had. That aspect of humility is important to inculcate.

The act of telling someone what we experienced is like boosting our ego. Ego drives us to want to tell someone because we think it is due to some greatness in ourselves that we are having inner experiences or that we are more spiritual than they are. We need to curb our ego. This is another reason that we have been asked not to talk about our inner spiritual experiences.

Q: *Is there any reason that rising above the body in meditation would be harmful or dangerous for us to do?*

Meditation has never hurt anyone and never will hurt anyone – especially those who have been initiated into the Mysteries of the Beyond by a perfect living Master. Meditation can not be harmful or dangerous to us. We have the guidance of the Master overhead. Our Master is always taking care of us.

As we meditate, we reach a calmer state. We become peaceful human beings. We become more loving. We actually are taking steps towards our goal. There is a transformation that happens from within, not because of our reading or listening to a lecture, but because of the experience of seeing and hearing the divine Light and Sound of God. If we do not meditate, we can not have that experience. That meditation experience is definitely going to help us.

There is nothing to fear about meditation. Sometimes the words "rising above physical body-consciousness," make people think that our soul is going up and we may wonder, "What happens if the soul goes up and never comes back into the body?" But in meditation, that is not the case. When we say "rising above physical body-consciousness," we are not talking about physically leaving the body. We are talking about shifting our attention into higher states of consciousness: from the physical to the astral, from the astral to the causal, from the causal to the supracausal, and from the supracausal to the region of all Truth, God Itself. These regions are not up in the sky; they are all within ourselves. They are occurring concurrently with this physical region in which our body resides. They are beyond time and space. Please do not be afraid. As you sit for meditation, sit with a prayer to God that says, "O God, give us whatever is best for us." Then we can receive whatever God feels is best. It is under God's will that we are all in this world and God will give us what is best for us.

The great saints say that even when a leaf moves, it is because of God's will, since everything was created by God. As we meditate, we should be sitting with loving remembrances of God. We should be sitting with a prayer in our heart and soul to have God give us whatever is best for us. Then, as Sant Darshan Singh Ji Maharaj would poetically say, we would sit as an empty cup and let God pour in all the sweet nectar that God wants us to drink. As we sit for meditation, we will have experiences of bliss, joy, and happiness. Those are states that take us far, far away from the states of jealousy, competition, and fear. Within ourselves is a treasure house filled with love and bliss.

Q: *Where are the inner realms?*

When we withdraw our attention to the single eye, we become absorbed in the inner Light and Sound. Then, after we meet the radiant form of the Master and rise above body-consciousness, we find inner realms. These inner dimensions or realms exist concurrently with our physical universe. For lack of better terminology, we speak of inner and outer, or higher and lower regions. These terms are not exactly descriptive because we are talking about states of consciousness. They do not exist in time and space, but we have the illusion that our physical world is in time and space. The physical region with the earth, sun, planets, and galaxies exists simultaneously with spiritual regions. We measure time and space in this physical universe because that is the only frame of reference that we know. But all these regions, from the physical to the spiritual, exist as states of consciousness. When we talk about traveling to inner or higher regions, we are not actually traveling anywhere or going up or in. We are actually refocusing our attention to a different state of consciousness or awareness.

Q: *Does Sant Mat help one develop supernatural powers such as* riddhis *and* siddhis *or is it mainly focused on God-realization?*

There are many yogic ways. *Ida* is the left way; *sushmana* is the middle way; and *pingala* is the right way. Through many yogic practices, people go into ida and pingala. When you are on those paths, you can gain what people would think of as supernatural powers. In the East, they are called *riddhis* and *siddhis*. Through rigorous practices, one can attain those states. But the path of Sant Mat does not focus on attaining supernatural powers for the following reason: when we get those powers, we want to use them. As we use them, we are entangling ourselves in lower states, rather than soaring into the higher realms of consciousness.

Another factor is that it takes many years to perfect the riddhis and siddhis. What are the results of all that effort? We are spending years, and maybe our whole lifetime, perfecting the development of supernatural powers to perform feats with the mind that any person can do with his or her physical body normally. Some people may spend years trying to do astral projection so they can look at their body from a vantage point in their room, or so they can move about outside without their physical body. But what have you gained? You can see your body in a mirror in one second's time and walk outside to see the environment in a minute. By spending years to do that, you have used up time that you may have spent in journeying to inner regions and attaining union with God which cannot be found by riddhis and siddhis.

Some people may spend their lifetime trying to perform miracles with the power of mind that one can do normally with one's own body. For example, you may spend forty years to perfect the art of having something material such as a coin or a spoon manifest. But all we need to do is reach into our pocket to pull out a coin or open a kitchen drawer for a spoon. While people may find it remarkable that someone can do this out of thin air, what was the gain for the person who spent a lifetime perfecting those riddhis or siddhis? A mere coin or spoon? How will that help him or her find God?

For example, there is a story of the yogi who spent his whole life perfecting the act of walking on water. When he came to a river the ferryman asked if he would like him to take him across the river for a penny. The yogi replied that he could do so himself. The yogi spent a long time preparing himself with all kinds of rites and rituals to walk on the river. After many hours, he finally set out to walk on the water. He thought he would receive praise and admiration for this act from the ferryman, but received none. The ferryman asked how long it took him to perfect this feat. The yogi told him it took him many years to learn how to walk on water. The ferryman then said, "I could have taken you across for one penny and in less time!"

What is the actual benefit that the yogi gained other than to show off and boost his ego that he could use supernatural powers? The actual act of going across the river could have been done by a boatman without his having spent his whole lifetime in learning how to do that. The yogi could have made better use of his life to journey instead across the river of life to find God.

We need to decide what is the best use of our time. Walking on water, flying in the air, or manifesting physical objects are events that still take place only in the physical realm. We want to enjoy finding the higher spiritual realms and attaining communion with the Lord. When the end of our life comes, do we want to have the ability to know where our soul will go after death and to return to the Lord so we do not have to return to the cycle of births and deaths, or do we want to have attained miraculous powers such as walking on water or manifesting a physical object, which will be of no help to our soul?

The path of Sant Mat is the path that takes us back to God on the sushmana nadi. This is the middle way that goes all the way up to Sach Khand, or the highest spiritual region in which the soul merges back into God and has God-realization. For this we need to connect with the Shabd or Naam within, which is not audible to the outer ear. The Naam is only audible to our inner ear. As our sensory currents collect at the single eye, called the seat of the soul, then we experience the divine Light and Sound or Music of God within ourselves.

It is a question of being able to still the body and mind, and then, with help and grace, we can experience our soul. Rather than spending time developing supernatural powers, which will not help us rise above these lower regions to attain communion with God, it is a better use of our human life to attain self-knowledge and God-realization.

Q: *Should we want to gain psychic powers from meditation?*

Those who set goals for spiritual practice are not interested in gaining riddhis and siddhis, psychic powers of telepathy in which one reads the thoughts of another, transvision in which one sees what is happening somewhere else, or seeing the past and future, or having other powers. But as a by-product of shifting one's attention from the physical realm to any other state of consciousness, these powers occur naturally. Those engaged in trying to reach the highest spiritual goal of union with God do not wish to waste time pursuing or using these psychic powers. Although these powers may come to them naturally, they are nothing more than the ability to shift one's attention to other states of consciousness. We can look at it this way. God is everything and everywhere. God is the state of all-consciousness. God is aware of everything that is, from the smallest microbe to the entire physical universe to all realms of creation. Thus, the soul is a part of God and when it identifies itself with God it has the same all-consciousness.

Telepathy is but a small ability to shift one's attention into knowing another's thoughts. Transvision is shifting one's attention to view another physical location far away. Seeing the past is shifting attention to the states of consciousness in which all that has happened is recorded. Knowing the future is basically only knowing the karmic reactions that are to come, but does not allow someone to know what free will someone will choose. We can only know the seventy-five percent laid out because that too is recorded in other states of consciousness as the karmic destiny of a particular person. We can know the trends of the seventy-five percent but not what he or she will do with that free will. That is why going to a fortune teller to read the future can never be fully accurate, because they may be sensitive to the broad karmic events due to happen, but those events are always surrounded by a person's free choice that can not be predicted. If someone initiated by a perfect spiritual Master goes to a fortune teller, the Master has already taken over the disciple's karmic accounts and helps the disciple wind up the karma in the  best possible way. A fortune teller would not know how that Master will adjust that person's karma, so the fortune teller can not be completely accurate.

Spiritually enlightened beings have access to telepathy or knowing the past and part of the future because they can easily shift their attention to other states in which these are known. Although they can do so, they do not use these powers. They are a waste of time. When the goal is to reunite the soul with God, why do we want to watch the television programming of someone else's thoughts, or someone else's past lives or future? We have enough problems with knowing our own thoughts, or our own past, let alone wasting time in trying to read other people's problems. Our goal is to stop thinking about our own thoughts and start tuning into the unbelievable bliss and joy that occur when we could have a romance with God. Who wants to bother with tuning into someone else's problems or thoughts when we could be having nuptial wedlock with God!

When he was a child, Sant Kirpal Singh Ji Maharaj had powers of transvision and could see what was happening in other locations. One day as a child at school, he suddenly had transvision that his grandmother was dying. He told the teacher that he wanted to go home at once to be with his grandmother, as he knew she was suddenly dying. The teacher thought it was the ploy of a mischievous child to get out of school. She would not let him go. During the school day a message came from home to let young Kirpal Singh go home as his grandmother had died. Sant Kirpal Singh Ji knew he had suchlike powers, but he prayed to God to take these powers away from him. He did not want them to interfere with his true goal of finding God.

We must choose the area into which we wish to put time and effort. We can spend our whole life trying to gain transvision of events in this world, which we can easily find out by making a phone call or turning on the television. We can spend our whole life gaining telepathic powers, when we can easily ask someone what they are thinking. These feats may make us feel we have gained something, but in the end, they do not lead us to God. But if we spend our time learning how to shift our consciousness to the realm of God, then we have gained everything there is to gain and know everything there is to know. We will know for certain that we are immortal, that we will live on after our physical demise, and that we will be bathed in eternal bliss. Which achievement do you think is more valuable?

When we learn to make choices about where to put our attention, we can shift our focus to God. We will find that we will not need to waste time dabbling in lower powers. Exploring lower regions such as the astral or causal will not hold our interest for they too are distractions just as the physical plane is. Instead, we will want to reach the highest source of bliss and happiness – being one with God. If we multiply all the ecstasy, joy, and happiness we have in this world by the power of ten, hundreds, thousands, or millions we will not even have an inkling of the bliss awaiting us when we merge back in God. When we taste that bliss, nothing in any lower regions, including psychic powers, will attract us anymore.

 Q: Is there a difference between the Master coming to us in a dream, a vision, or in meditation? If, in a dream, we are not awake or conscious enough to do simran to test the Master's form by repeating the five Charged Names, then how can we know if it is really

the Master's form? Is seeing the Master in the dream state really the Master or just a dream?

When we see the Master in meditation and test the form with the five Charged Names, we can be sure that it is the Master who has appeared to us. When we are not meditating, but suddenly the Master comes in vision while we are awake and conscious, we can test the form with the five Charged Names. If it stands, then it is the Master. Visions can come when we are not meditating but suddenly the Master's form appears before us while our eyes are open, or he appears before us within while we were in the middle of doing something else. Sometimes when we are about to fall asleep, or when we just get up, and are consciously awake but not meditating, the Master can appear to us in vision. A vision is not a dream, though, because in a vision we are conscious.

A dream takes place when we are not conscious but in the sleep state, and we are getting impressions from our subconscious mind. There is no way of knowing whether a dream was true or not, whether it was a dream of the Masters or any other dream. The dream is a process in which our subconscious mind is sending some information to us. There is no way of verifying our dream. If we have dreams about the Master, then they are good signs because at least even when we are sleeping, we are focused in the right area. But there is nothing to confirm whether a dream was right or wrong, because a dream is a dream anyway. It is a fiction. No one can verify anything that is fiction. But visions are different, because you have them in your waking state. In a vision, because you are awake, you can test the form with the five Charged Names and if the form is of the positive Power it will remain.

I would say that when you are sleeping and have a dream that makes you happy, or dreams about the Masters, generally it makes you feel good when you get up. Although they are good dreams to have,

there is no way of knowing whether it was the Master or your mind, because everything coming in the dream is from your mind. It is only when we move from the sleep and dream state to a conscious state in which we can test the Master's form with the five Charged Names and it stands before us that we can say for sure that it is the Master.

Q: What should we do if, in meditation, we hear the Master telling us something, but we do not see him? Should we listen to the advice?

The Masters tell us that if any voice speaks to us during meditation, we should not pay attention to it but ask it to present itself to us so we can see it. Then we can test it with the five Charged Words. If the form is of the positive Power, it will remain before us. If it is a form of the negative Power, then it will go away after the repetition of the five Names.

Q: Can we ever see the Master manifest with our eyes open without meditating?

Yes, we definitely can. Everything in the inner regions is occurring concurrently with this region. If our attention is focused we can see the Light, hear the Sound, or see the radiant form of the Master with eyes and ears opened or closed. The reason we close our eyes is to shut off the outside lights so we can concentrate more easily. By closing our eyes, we prevent our inner gaze from being distracted by outer lights. But when we advance, and sometimes out of special grace at any stage, the Master will show himself in radiant form to us with our eyes open. There are times when the Master can even physically manifest to the disciple while the Master's physical body is thousands of miles away. It is a matter of the attention of the disciple and grace from the Master. Again, we always test the form with the repetition of the five Charged Names to make sure the form is of the positive Power and, if it is, that form will remain.

Q: Is it karma or other factors that determine whether we have the radiant form of the Master appear on a regular basis each day? Since it is said in the teachings of the Master that the Master's form comes of its own accord, is there anything we can do to help that process?

As a disciple it helps to first lead an ethical life in which the virtues of truthfulness, humility, selfless service, chastity or purity, and nonviolence are inculcated. We need to lead a life in harmony with the will of God. Our daily thoughts, words, and deeds affect the karma our soul has to pay in the future. Ethical living is good because it keeps us from having turmoil in our system and reduces the fluctuations of the mind so we can be calm and still when we meditate. It is important to lead a loving, harmonious life, in which we help and care for others. Ethical life, then, is one factor that speeds up our inner progress so we can reach the radiant form of the Master within.

Another important factor is to have a ruling passion to know God. Without that, we are not able to reach our goal. In this world, if we want to attain something, we need to be totally focused on it. Similarly, if we want our soul to enter inner spiritual regions to find God, we need to be passionately in love with God. We need to be totally focused on God. At every moment of our existence, all our thoughts, words, and deeds should be imbued with the love of God. If we lead that kind of life then, when we sit for meditation, it will be easier to still our mind. As our mind becomes stilled, we are preparing for the radiant form of the Master to appear to guide us in the higher spiritual regions.

Our part is to be in a state in which that radiant form can lift us within. Our job is to lead an ethical life that is loving and caring, to regularly do our spiritual practices of meditation accurately to still the mind, and to be absorbed into the Light and Sound of God. As we still the body and mind, the radiant form automatically appears. If we are distracted as we meditate – and the distraction may come from many places – from lack of ethical living, outer temptations, or inaccurate meditations, then we are not going to be able to reach our goal.

Our goal as human beings is to connect with the power of God. For that to happen we must become absorbed in the inner Light and Sound. Then, the radiant form of the Master appears as our inner guide to take us on the inner journey back through higher planes until we reach our eternal Home, God. As we make ourselves receptive to and totally focused on God, then it will be easy to find stillness and calmness in the turmoil around us. As we find that stillness within, the radiant form will automatically appear. As disciples our only job is to reach the radiant form, which will then lead us into the inner spiritual regions. Initiates and those on the spiritual quest trying to reach God need to lead an ethical life, have a ruling passion for God, and be receptive. Each moment of our life should be imbued with the love of God.

Sant Mat is not a path of negation of life. We are not supposed to leave the world to meditate as recluses in a cave, forest, or jungle. We are to develop spiritually while attending to our worldly responsibilities to family, job, education, and commitments as citizens. But as we go through life and perform our obligations to the best of our ability, our attention should remain focused on God. In Punjabi there is a saying which means, "Our hands to our work, but our hearts to the Beloved." We need to pass through life in the best possible manner, but while doing so, our attention should be totally focused on God. As we find that focus in our life, then it is not difficult to reach the radiant form who will then guide us into the inner spiritual regions.

Q: When we go within through Shabd meditation do we only see our own Master inside, or can we also see other past Masters within?

As we meditate and pass through the various Lights, the inner sky, stars, moon and sun we reach the radiant form of the Master. We meet the radiant form of the Master who has initiated us, because it is his responsibility to take care of those whom he has initiated. One of the benefits that an initiate has is that at the time of death it is the radiant form of the Master who initiated us who comes for us. It is not the Angel of Death who comes for the initiated soul. It is the responsibility of the Master who initiated us to take care of us. When we meditate and reach the radiant form of our Master, he guides us into the inner spiritual regions. Once we are on the inner planes, it is not that we will only meet one Master, but we can meet other past Masters of Sant Mat also. Depending on our journey and what the Master decides is the fastest route for us to get back to God, we can encounter or meet other Masters as well within.

Q: How can we make spiritual progress in meditation with all the confusion and stress in life?

Often in life, we can not understand why things do not happen according to the way we would like them to happen. We feel happy when everything goes according to what we want, but when things happen contrary to our desires, there is turmoil in our life. Confusion and turmoil are a part of life.

In this age of advanced transportation and telecommunication, we come in contact with more people, including those who are different from us. With each interaction, we receive different input into our systems. Our great-great-grandfathers who were living perhaps by tilling the land may have seen only one, two, or three people beyond their family the whole day. Life was easier, in one sense, because people only had to deal with a few other people. But in today's world, we might deal with hundreds of other people every day. When we go to work, we may sit on a train with hundreds of people. If we drive in a car, we may pass hundreds of people on the road. If we turn on the television, we receive input from people on many channels, plus hearing news about millions of people around the world. Input is coming from many directions, adding to the confusion and turmoil.

When we meditate we experience calm. The beauty of meditation is that the peace we experience during meditation lingers beyond that time as well. The benefits of meditation last with us afterward so that our reactions to our surroundings, and the input that comes to us, can remain calm. Then, whatever turmoil is there, our reaction can be peaceful, and we can apply balm to the situation so it does not escalate. Therefore, no matter in what situation we find ourselves, through meditation we can deal with it in a more peaceful manner.

Whenever there is turmoil in our surroundings we are perturbed and it causes unhappiness. As soon as we connect with the Light and Sound of God, we will experience peace within and recognize our connection with the Divine. The strength of being connected with the Divine gives us peace. As we find ourselves at peace, our reactions to the turmoil of the environment remain calmer.

To think that all our problems will go away is wishful thinking. Let us take a couple of examples. Suppose we are seriously ill or have a big financial problem. If we think that if we meditate the illness or the financial problem will go away, then we are deluding ourselves. But there is a benefit to meditation in these situations. What happens is that, even though the problem is there, our reaction to the problem is different. We start looking at the situation with a different point of view or angle of vision. Then, the situation does not trouble us as much. To illustrate this, we know that sometimes the same problem can trouble one person much more than another. Similarly, we can face the same situation at two different times in our life, but it may trouble us more at one time than at another. How we react to the same situation is due to how we feel at the time. Meditation calms us so that the effects of whatever turmoil is around us are minimized, causing our thinking to become clearer.

The key is to understand that our true existence is at the level of our soul. Our soul is on this journey back to God. If we think that through meditating we are not going to have any problems in life, then we are not being realistic. Problems come because of past karmas. We all have karmas associated with us. We have sanchit karma or storehouse karma, which started from the day our soul separated from God. We have been through many existences, and in each we collected karma that went into the storehouse karma. Out of that storehouse, a portion is taken, which is called the pralabdh karma, through which we have to pass in this lifetime. That is the karma that we as human beings sometimes do not understand. For example, suppose there is a young person who is loving, kind, and caring and seems to do everything right, bringing happiness and joy to his or her family and community. Then, suddenly, that loving person has a terrible illness and suffers a great amount. Others cannot understand how someone who is so nice could be in that kind of a situation. We are not aware of the karma associated with others or ourselves. Many times in life, we cannot logically or analytically decipher everything that happens to us. Why do some people, who may be good, die young in life? The question of why bad things happen to people who are good is one that often arises. We have to pass through the pralabdh karma in life, but meditation can help us deal with it in a calmer and more peaceful manner.

Once we realize that this life is only a passing phase, we will also realize that whatever state we are in must pass, too. Then, even if there is turmoil, it will not affect us. There is an interesting story from the life of a king. There was a king who told the ministers running his cabinet, "I have ups and downs in life. Some days I am happy, and some days I am depressed. I want you to find a solution that will keep me in equipoise so that my days of distress do not bother me and my days of happiness do not elate me so much that I lose contact with the true reality."

They worked on this problem, searching to find something that would keep the king in equipoise in all situations. They met together and thought of an idea. They then put a gift for the king in a package and brought it to him.

The ministers said, "This is going to help you in all situations." They asked the king to open the gift. When the king opened it he saw a ring.

They told him, "You must wear the ring." So he put it on his finger. When he did so, he saw writing on the ring. He read the inscription that said, "This, too, shall pass." The ministers explained that this saying should remind him in times of trouble that those moments would pass and he would return to smooth sailing. It would also remind him in times of elation that those moments, too, would pass and not to be down-hearted when those joyous times ended. In this way, he could remember that the ups and downs of life will all pass, and that he should maintain his equilibrium at all times.

When we meditate we find calmness so that during times of elation and trouble we can realize that all this shall pass. In this way, we can deal with life in a happier and more balanced way. The key is to be calm, still, and peaceful inside. If we do not learn how to do this, we will experience more turmoil, not only in our lives, but also as we bring it into the lives of others. If we expect that others are going to behave the way we want them to behave, we are mistaken. We live in a free world today in which everyone says. "I can do whatever I want. Who are you to tell me any-thing?" Even children tell that to their parents. We are living in that kind of age today. We need to recognize that all situations will pass. Time is not going to stop. It is ticking away. The situation might linger on for a few seconds, a few hours, a few days, a few months, or a few years, but the sit-uation will definitely change. When a situation is beyond our control and brings difficulties, then remember that this time, also, shall pass. As we meditate, the stillness within helps us go through life with a courageous outlook so that nothing can bring us down.

We know that we are soul and a part of God. We are not distinct from God. We are one and the same. Why should we be afraid of anything? Why should we let anything bring turmoil into our lives? Just as saints in the East have described how the lotus flower lives in muddy water while its petals remain dry and clean, we too can live like that. We live in this world of *maya,* or illusion, that brings difficulties into our lives, but as we meditate, we too can be like the lotus flower so that we can remain peace-ful throughout the turbulent waters of life.

6 Receiving Spiritual Guidance

Q: What is the relationship between the physical Master and the Master Power? How does the Master provide protection to the disciple?

What helps and protects us is the Power of God. When we focus our attention on questions such as who are we, is there a God, and what is our relationship to God, then we will at least recognize that there is some Power controlling this world and that things are not happening haphazardly. Many things are happening in this universe out of our control. But that does not mean that they are happening by themselves. God, who created this world, has control over what happens. As we grow older and pass through different phases of our life, our faith in God starts to be strengthened.

When we need to learn a certain subject, our societies have a system in which we go to someone who is an expert who can teach us. That is the reason that we go to school. Otherwise, since we are all educated, why don't we all teach our own children? Most people send their children to school because we feel that one person might be an expert in physics; another might be an expert in chemistry; while a third might be an expert in history, geography, or some other subject. We send our children to teachers so that they can learn those subjects from experts in the different fields. Similarly, the role of the spiritual Master is to help people develop the spiritual aspects of our lives.

Human beings have three aspects. We have the physical aspect of our life, which includes our physical body and physical activities. We also have the mental or intellectual aspect of our lives. We use the mental aspect to think, learn, and make decisions at an intellectual level according to what makes the most sense to us. Most people do not develop more than their physical and intellectual sides. There is a third side – the spiritual aspect – on which few people focus. The role of the spiritual Master is to bring that aspect out in other human beings. The Master's job is to help us recognize that we are soul and are a part of God. The Master does this through helping us invert our attention through meditation. Through meditating, our soul can transcend consciousness of this physical world and journey through inner spiritual regions until it reaches its Source, God.

The Master serves as our guide and companion on this journey. First, we journey to the astral region in which we have an astral body and astral mind. Then, we travel to the causal plane in which we have a causal body and causal mind. After crossing these three lower regions of the physical, astral, and causal planes, we shed the physical, astral, and causal coverings and reach the fourth region or supra-causal plane. It is here that we recognize that we are soul, with only a thin layer covering our soul. Finally, we reach the stage of Sach Khand, or region of Truth, in which all coverings are shed. There, we experience ourselves as soul and merge back in God. At that stage we have firsthand realization that there is a power that helps and guide us.

The Masters of Sant Mat have been teaching that the Power of God works through some human pole. Human beings learn from other human beings. Since we are used to learning through our physical senses, and since God is spirit, we need the help of a teacher who is at a physical level. That Power works through a human pole so we can have someone from whom we can learn. But it is not the physical form of the Master that is helping us. Irrespective of which human pole it is, it is actually the Power of God that helps and guides us. It needs some human form, because if there were none, we would not be able to recognize it. The reason that saints and Masters come into the world is to talk to us at our own level. They live in our societies so we have a chance to see and learn from how they live and what they do. Yet, it is not the physical body of the Master that helps us. We think it is their outer form helping us because we only see the physical body of the Master. Yet, that physical body does not do anything for us. It is only the Power of God working through that body that helps us. That is the reason that in Sant Mat, time and time again, Masters tell us to connect with the Power of God. Let us not connect ourselves to the body of the Master, because that body is also going to deteriorate. We need to connect to the Power of God working through the human pole.

As we meditate and concentrate on the inner Light, we pass through inner vistas of Lights, sky, stars, moon, and sun to reach the radiant or ethereal form of the Master. The radiant form serves as our inner guide, protecting us on our journey as he takes us back to God. The physical body of the Master becomes a mouthpiece of that Power. Therefore, the real Master is not the physical body; it is the Power of God. That is what really protects us and takes us back to our Eternal Home.

Q: How should we view the Master?

It is important to understand that what we call "the Master" is not the physical body of the Master. Our Master, our guide, is the Power of God. In this world we need to have some reference that we can understand because we, as human beings, have never seen God with these physical eyes or heard God with these physical ears. To recognize that the Power of God is helping us we, as human beings, find it easier to recognize a face as our guide. When we are initiated we can recognize the face of the physical form of the Master. Then, as we meditate, we recognize that face as the inner radiant form of the Master through whom the Power of God is working. It is not that the physical body is God or the Master. It is the Power of God that is our Master or guide. The physical body is there just for guidance. We can take the physical form of the Master as a guide, or as an elder brother who helps us, but it is God who helps us. It is the Power of God that guides us in the inner regions.

Q. If we are initiated and have great love for the Master, we sometimes would like this spirituality to spill over to those who we love who might not be initiated. For example, my parents are not initiated, but I often think, "Wouldn't it be good if the blessings of my Master were upon them?" Is the grace of the Master extended to those who we love even if they are not initiated?

The Masters have said clearly that once we are initiated, not only is the grace of the Masters coming to us, but also it extends to help our near and dear ones, our loved ones, our relatives, our friends, and people with whom we are close. That is how help is provided to many people, not only in our families, but also people we love with whom we come in contact.

Q. How can we make the adjustment from times that we are with the Master to times when we are away from the Master? It seems that the more time I spend with the Master, the more meaningless everyday life without him becomes. I know that Master wants us to observe positive mysticism and fulfill our duties to our family, careers, and society, but it is so blissful and intoxicating to be with the Master that everything else in life pales in comparison and seems to lose its charm.

I actually think there is no adjustment to make because whether we are physically with the Master or not, the Master is always with us. It is a recognition of the fact that the Power of God is always there helping us. The Masters have told us that the day we get initiated, the radiant form of the Master is sitting within us at the seat of the soul. When we are in the physical presence of the Master, and our attention is on the Master, that helps to guide our attention to God. Saints have written about the benefits of being in the physical presence because it helps us focus on God, the most important aspect of our lives.

Life is such that physically we can not be in the physical presence of the Master at all times. We have jobs to do. This is not a path of renunciation that asks us to leave our societies and homes and physically park ourselves at the feet of the Master, even though some of us would like to do that. The path of Sant Mat says that we need to live in the world. We need to discharge our responsibilities and take care of our obligations. We live according to what Sant Darshan Singh Ji Maharaj called a path of "positive mysticism." This means that we try to excel in all spheres of life, but while attending to day-to-day chores, our attention is focused on God. This is where simran helps. When we do simran, we are remembering God. We are repeating God's Name. We are focusing our attention on God. That is also what we are doing when we are in the physical presence of the Master. When our attention is on the Master, it is drawing our attention towards God.

The Master is not that physical body; it is the Power of God working through that human pole. It is that Power of God to which we are attracted. It is not the physical form of the Master to which we are attracted. It is the loving, illuminating, and all-encompassing Power of God working through the human pole that attracts us. It is

not attracting us to the body of the Master. It is attracting us to God, to that divine Power.

God is a creative force. The Bible says, "In the beginning was the Word, and the Word was with God, and the Word was God" (John 1:1). God and the holy Word are one and the same. It is a spiritual force or vibration that is at the heart of all creation, which brought everything into existence. That is actually what the Master or the Master Power is. It is our attraction to that enrapturing and magnetic Power that draws us towards it. That is the pull we find in the physical presence of the Master. As we spend enough time in meditation, we start to recognize that pull on a daily basis. That attraction is there every moment of our life.

The saints have said that we should reach a stage where we close our eyes and see the radiant form of the Master. The only reason we see the radiant form of the Master through whom we received initiation is because we need to recognize that Power in some form, because in the human body we can only recognize what we have experienced through our eyes and ears. Therefore, the Power takes the form of the body of the Master so we can recognize that Power of God. This is the reason that, as we meditate, we are asked to reach the state where we can experience that radiant form, where we are able to converse with that radiant form, where we are able to ask questions of that radiant form and receive answers.

Sant Darshan Singh Ji Maharaj would often say that this radiant form becomes our companion, our unpaid counselor. Every time we need some information or a question answered, or we are in a jam and need help with our difficult lives, we can pop right back within through meditation, ask the question, receive the answer, and bingo, we can go forward. We need to reach that stage. We can attain that stage when we meditate, become receptive, make our life loving and caring, and inculcate ethical virtues. Thus, as a seeker or a disciple on the way back to God, we need to communicate with this Power of God. Once that happens, then we do not feel any separation between the physical presence of the Master and ourselves. We then recognize the Power of God at all times.

Q: The path of Sant Mat teaches that the living Master is commissioned by God. Do the Masters who leave this physical life have to return here for another life? If not, where do the perfect souls come from to reincarnate in the human form?

The Masters have said that God sends God's sons or daughters – or whatever term by which we may call them in this day and age – to come and help souls return to God. Kabir Sahib, who shaped Sant Mat in its present modern form over five hundred years ago, has described how this creation came into being. There was a devotee, named Kal, who had done much penance and through great effort won God's grace. God was happy with Kal, and in God's wisdom, granted Kal three boons for these penances. Kal wanted to rule a kingdom. Up to that point, Kabir Sahib tells us that there were only two regions of creation: Sach Khand, made of pure spirit, and Par Brahm, made of spirit with a thin veil of illusion. When Kal wanted a region, these three lower regions came into being: the causal region, a region of spirit mixed with equal parts matter; the astral region, a region of spirit with more matter; and the physical region, in which we live, which is predominately matter with only a small amount of spirit. Kal was given jurisdiction over these three lower regions. Souls that were separated from God were then sent to these regions. When souls came to these regions they were only allowed by Kal to cycle back and forth in the lower regions according to the law of karma that was established. As this law of karma was set up, Kal asked for three boons: one, that when the souls left the human body, it would not immediately return to God; two, that the embodied souls would forget their true Home in God in Sach Khand, and that they would forget their previous lives; and three, it God wanted any soul to return to God, God could not take it back by showing miracles; rather, God would have to assume the human form and take the soul back through the process of satsang or spiritual discourses. Thus, if we are in one form and do not remember our previous life, then we are not going to remember the one before that or the one before that or before that. Therefore, we are finally going to forget God.

When God gave Kal these boons, it was clear that none of the souls would be able to go back to God, because if we did not remember from where we came, it would be difficult to ever return there. We can go here, here, here, and here, but we will never know where to go back. This next part of the deal was that if God wanted to bring the souls back – and Kal knew God could bring them back any time that God wanted to – that God would not take the souls back through a miracle by which all of a sudden everyone returned immediately to God. According to Kabir Sahib and the teachings of the Sant Mat tradition, this third boon was given because God extracted a concession so there would be an opportunity for separated souls to go back to God. That concession was that God would have to come down to the lower regions through a representative in a human form to take back the separated souls. It is only in the human form that the faculties to know oneself and know God would be provided. The only way God could take souls back was to work through a human form and talk like others to take the souls back through the process of satsang. Through satsang, the Power of God could help bring those souls back to their true home.

Satsang is made of two terms: "sat" means "Truth" and "sang" means "gathering, or in the company of." "Satsang" means "being in the company of Truth." Satsang includes being in the physical presence of the Master, listening to the teachings, receiving initiation, meditating, and leading an ethical life so the soul can go back to God. God could not take souls back through miracles, but had to work through a human pole who would make the teachings, and the way back to God, known to souls through the process of satsang.

Those souls chosen to come in the form of what we call the Master, or the human pole through which the Power of God works, are coming from the highest of the regions, the truly spiritual region.

When these souls come into the human body from the highest of these regions, which are the subtlest of the subtle regions, two things can happen. When we look at history, we find that many great saints and mystics have said that they came first as one person, and in another age they came in another human form, and in still another age they came in another human body. Those saints were coming back as saints again and again. Then there are others who came once in a human body and returned to God. There is no fixed rule that a saint has to come ten times or twenty times or once or twice or any number of times. It depends on whosoever God feels would be appropriate to send.

When we read the scriptures, we find references in which some saints have said that they came right from God's home and are going back. That is one kind of reference in the scriptures. There are other references in the scriptures which say, for example, "I was Kabir Sahib. I was Guru so and so, and I was so and so in these lifetimes." Some saints have also said that they were sent directly from God, and whatever they speak is not of themselves but is coming from God. We find these different situations that the great saints and mystics have talked about in their writings regarding how they have come into this world.

According to the will of God, any one of these souls from the highest of the highest region who have merged in God can be sent by God to come here in the human body. Sant Darshan Singh Ji Maharaj used to say that they are sent here and act like us, eat with us, drink with us, laugh with us, cry with us, and live with us so that we are able to understand them and learn from them. We generally can only learn from someone who speaks the same language that we do. If we only know English and if someone comes and starts talking Hindi or Sanskrit or German, we are not going to understand them. To know about the spiritual way, we need someone in the human form who can talk in our own language to teach us a method to experience something within and who can give us that experience as well. It is not through talking and reading that we gain spiritually. It is only through firsthand spiritual experience that one gains. These souls, called saints and Masters, come into the human form to help us recognize the way back to God through firsthand spiritual experience. According to the Sant Mat tradition, each Master who comes here comes with a fixed number of initiates that he is going to take back with him. This is where the expression from scriptures comes from that the "shepherd knows his sheep" that we also find referred to in the writings in the Sant Mat tradition.

Q. Once an initiate reaches the highest plane of Sach Khand, does this attainment of perfection somehow "obligate" that disciple to reincarnate and become a living Master in gratitude in a future birth?

As we rise above the physical body and go through various regions we merge in our Master and finally reach Sach Khand where we merge in God. When we attain that state of merger we are in a state of bliss. It is not necessary that having attained that state we would be sent back to this physical world. For these great Masters, coming back here is a difficult chore. Yet, these souls do come back out of love and compassion and obedience to God. The word "obedience" is used often, especially in the scriptures of the East. When souls attain merger with God, they are in a state of bliss, divine love, and ecstasy, and none of these souls wants to come back to these lower regions, but since there is a job to be done, someone has to do it. Generally you give the job to the best person, so it is done properly. Let us say you want something new to be designed. If you are running a company or a corporation, you are going to find the best people that, according to your intelligence, you can put together as a team to get the job done. Generally, we always want the best people to do whatever job needs to be done. God also tries to send those who God feels will get the job done. It is not necessary that we come back. There are many souls that do return to God, but few of them come back to this world. It is not necessary that an initiate who goes back to God would be coming back down here to this world.

As an example from this world, I would say this would be like jury duty. All of a sudden in your mail you find a letter. It says, "You have been selected as a juror." You can not say, "No." You can go there and reply to their questions and if they do not like your answers, they may say, "We do not need you. Go back home." Although it is not like that regarding the question of coming back to this world, it is similar. In jury duty our name gets picked up by a computer or someone picks our name, and we get a letter in the mail. Irrespective of our beliefs, we do not know what case we are going to get. Something similar happens when God sends a soul back to earth to bring separated souls back to God. It is not necessary that everyone will become a juror. Many people go through a lifetime and never have to go through jury duty. For souls who merge back in God, it is not necessary that they will come back for another birth.

Q. If the Master Power is not the body, and the Power of the previous Masters is in the present living Master, then is Mastership a form of "divine channeling" if you will?

The word channeling is used very loosely in this day and age. Someone says that they are a channel for healing: physical healing, mental healing, emotional healing, or spiritual healing. Another person might say that he or she is a channel for such-and-such spirit, or that such and such spirit is channeling through him or her. What is interesting in this concept of the Master found in the Sant Mat tradition is that there is the Power of God working through a human pole. But that Power of God is also in each of us. Thus, the concept of channeling is that the Power is here as the Master Power, and the one who needs to be helped is our soul, and the Master is what is called the channel. The channel is used to bring the Power of God to the soul. But in Sant Mat, the physical form of the Master is not important. It is important only because when we are in the physical presence of the Master, we receive grace and our attention goes to God, but there are multi-dimensional manifestations of that Power

which does not happen in channeling. For example, in Sant Mat there are many manifestations of the Master Power. The physical body of the Master could be sitting in Europe or in India or in any part of the world, and the Power of God could be helping someone else thousands and thousands of miles away. The process of channeling is that the physical channel needs to be at one place and it is only at that time and instant that the power of whatever is being channeled is going to happen to you, such as a healing, whereas in the Sant Mat tradition, the Power of God is working through the human pole and can do so from thousands of miles away.

Saints have said, "Go to the lotus feet of a Master. Go and be in the physical presence of the Master." Why? because the atmosphere there is conducive to focusing on God. We recognize that we live in a world of many distractions. It is difficult to focus on God because we have forgotten what our previous lives were. We do not even recognize that we are a part of God. When we are in the physical presence of a Master, our attention goes to God. In that atmosphere we talk about God, make references to God, and focus on God.

There are other aspects of the Master's grace in Sant Mat. There is the grace of having spirituality pass through the eyes of the Master to us. According to Sant Mat, one-third of spirituality comes from word of mouth and two-thirds of spirituality comes to us through radiation, such as through the eyes of the Master. We receive spiritual radiation from being in the physical presence of the Master and having his *darshan*. What is darshan? It is difficult to explain in words. It is like being able to capture the radiation coming in our direction. If we are in the physical presence of a Master and radiation is going here, there, up, down, and wherever else, and we are in that vicinity, it is easy to catch. But it is not limited to the physical presence of the Master, because the Power of God can manifest in many places. We do not have to be only in the physical presence as in channeling.

If someone is having an operation in Austria, while someone else is in an accident in Europe, and someone else is having a problem in Florida, the Master Power can provide help at the same time to all those people. According to Sant Mat, that is the difference between channeling and the help that we receive through the Power of God.

Q: When should I ask for guidance from the Master and when am I relying too heavily on him? For example, a couple of months ago I experienced extreme emotional pain, and I did not know what to do. So, during meditation, I had this inner urge to write a note to the Master asking for spiritual guidance. After the first draft, I decided to rewrite it in a solution mode, with gratefulness, and had faith that the situation would be solved. I was able to change my perception of the whole thing and the situation turned from being a painful event to one in which I could experience joy again. Was I leaning on the Master? Was I doing the right thing by changing my reaction to the situation?

The saints have always said that the Master is our best friend. As we meditate and truly concentrate and experience the radiant form of the Master within, that form becomes our unpaid counselor, as Sant Darshan Singh Ji Maharaj beautifully expressed it, and we can have guidance on the inside. That state is not easy to attain because our mind is always distracting us from going within. We are unable to understand our situation because we think and analyze based on our own knowledge basis, which is limited. When we pass through a difficult period, it is hard to understand why something unpleasant is happening to us.

There are three categories of people. At one extreme are those people who are truly evolved, who rise above physical body-consciousness, who experience the Master within, and whose faith is strong. They do not need to talk to anyone or do anything for help because they realize that all that is happening is under God's will. When our faith is really strong, we leave things to God, saying, "This is God's will; this is best for me." Then, we go forward from there. Later, we find out that it really was best for us. But not everyone is at that level. There are many stages at which we find ourselves.

There are many people who are at the other extreme, whose faith breaks easily. When things are going well, they are happy. When something is not going as they would like, they break. We become sad, have difficulties living our lives, and start to wonder, "Why is this happening to me?" Those are the people who might not even think about getting help and are repulsed from everything.

In the middle are many people who, if they have a chance to talk about their problems with the Master, feel that it relieves their pain. At the psychological level it relieves their pain because they know that they have told the Master everything. Those people are at that stage where their realization is not to the level where they think that God already knows everything.

Sant Darshan Singh Ji would often say that when we talk to the Master or God, we feel good about things. If we are far away from the Master, we may sit down to write a letter. Sant Darshan Singh Ji would also say that whether we post the letter or not, it gives us relief because our situation is helped. Depending on whatever we feel, all of these are good to do. There is nothing wrong in talking to the Master, and there is nothing wrong in writing to him. It depends on the level at which we are. Each one reacts differently given the same situation.

Many times we have seen people who live far away from the Master who have a problem. They write a letter—many have posted it and many have not even posted it—and the solution comes to them and things become easier. It appears that the difficulty disappeared. There are different stages through which we go.

One thing we should realize is that the Master is not the body. It is the Power of God. That Power of God helps us in whatever state we find ourselves. That Power of God is always there. It is not limited by buildings, cities, countries, or anything. This is the reason that we hear of people who experience many manifestations of the Master Power. We have heard examples from the life of Sant Kirpal Singh Ji 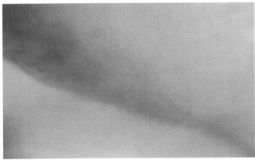 Maharaj that someone saw him helping him in one place when he was having an operation, while at the same time someone in another part of the world said he was taking care of his farm fields when someone came to rob the crops. Meanwhile, someone else in another part of the world experienced that manifestation at another place. That Power of God can have many manifestations. This is the all-knowing characteristic of that Power of God.

Other characteristics of the Power of God are being omnipotent and omnipresent – being all-powerful and being at every place, at all times – and can be experienced for ourselves. When we have an experience in our own life, then our faith in that Power of God is strengthened. When we do not have that experience for ourselves, but read about the experiences of others or hear about the experiences of others, it has an effect on our lives. That Power of God is there to help us in all situations.

We need to understand that we also have pralabdh karma associated with us, which is the karma through which we have to pass in this lifetime. Even though the sanchit karma is burned at the time of our initiation and is gone, the pralabdh karma is still associated with us because if that were taken over, then we would not be living anymore. Help is provided as we pass through our pralabdh karmas, but we do go through the ups and downs of life. It is not that we get initiated, and nothing of the outside world will affect us anymore. We still pass through the ups and downs of life, but help comes to us when we need help.

Saints have said that if a mountain is supposed to fall on us, that event is not totally changed or removed, but it feels only like a pin prick because help is provided by the Master Power. It is generally when we have the downs in life that we need help. When things are going well, we may even forget about God because we are so happy in whatever we are doing and do not even think about anything else. It is only when we have difficulties that we think and feel: "Why are we having these difficulties?" "How can we get out of it?" and "Why is this happening to us?" The mind then starts to play all kinds of games with us to depress us. Mind has many wiles by which it keeps us away from Reality. We must pass through the ups and downs of life. When our faith is strong, we can pass through those situations in a much easier and better manner. The help of the Master Power is always there, whether we know it or not.

We have heard of people who were in accidents who said they were going to fall, but the hand of the Master came and rescued them. We have heard experiences of those who went to a doctor who took an x-ray and found a cancerous growth. Then, they showed the x-ray to the Master. Two weeks later, they went back to the doctor who took another x-ray and found the growth was gone. The doctor could not figure out how that happened. These look like miracles, but it is actually help from the Master that comes to us. Masters do not perform miracles, but out of their compassion, grace flows. These are but a few examples. The faith of those who have had these experiences is strengthened because they received help. When those experiences happen to us, our faith is strengthened and nothing fazes us anymore. We know that even if it is a difficult period, it will pass away.

 Q: My question has two parts. First, what can we do when we do not have an opportunity to ask the Master something personally but have to make a decision and want to make sure it is for our spiritual growth and it is the best for us? The second question

is that the Master told me something and I could not follow his advice and now I feel sorry I did not take his advice. What can I do to forgive myself?

To answer the first question, many times it is not possible for us to be in the physical presence of our Master. The path of Sant Mat teaches that in those situations we should rely on the inner Master. When we get initiated, the radiant or the ethereal form of the Master is always at the single eye to give guidance in all spheres of life, whether physical, mental, emotional, or spiritual. As we meditate – and meditate properly – we are then able to withdraw our attention from the world outside and reach a state of no thoughts. We are able to collect our sensory currents at the seat of our soul and experience the Divine for ourselves. That radiant form within becomes our companion at all times. If we reach the state where we can get to that form, we find that form is with us twenty-four hours of the day. Just as we ask a question on the outside, we can ask our question on the inside. Many times, it is not easy to get to that state. Even though we might say that we have been practicing the path for a number of years, we are not able to concentrate well. When we have other activities in which we are involved in our life, it becomes difficult to concentrate properly. In those cases, I think we should all recognize that God is always with us. We have to use common sense. We have to use whatever knowledge we have and whatever we can find out about the situation in which we find ourselves. Then, we have to make the best possible call that we can and leave the rest in God's hands.

God's grace is with each of us at all times of the day and night. Irrespective of whether we are in one place or another, irrespective of whatever condition we are in, we should all realize that God is always there with us because our true self, the soul, is a part of God. It is not distinct from God. The difficulty in life is that we do not recognize the unity that we have with God, so we lead a life of duality. We think of ourselves as being apart, separated, and not united with God. But God is within us; our soul is a part of God. If we realize that, we will not experience any separation. When we get to that state of awareness, we recognize that all events happening in our lives are known by God. If we are not in the physical presence of the Master, we should realize that God is with us at all times, and we should make our best judgment call on a decision and go with it.

To answer your second question, many times when we ask a question, we have preconceived notions. We want a certain answer. Let us say there are three or four options. In our mind, we feel that one option is better for us and we want that confirmed, so we ask the question. We lay the options on the table. If the option suggested is the same that we wanted, we are happy. But if the option recommended is not what we thought it should be, we start to say, "But..." or "If..." and we start to list all the reasons for the option we want. We hedge around whichever answer we want to get. If we do that, then we should realize that our faith in getting the answer from whosoever we go to is not totally there. If we have faith in the Master, then we need to be open to the best of our capabilities to whatever answers come out to us. If we feel the answer is not in our best interest, I am sure we are never going to use it. Many times we do ask questions and are given a suggestion, but we put it aside because it does not meet what we want to do. Sometimes, when we go to the Masters, we want them to say yes to whatever we have decided so that it is approved. Then we can tell people that Master said this was okay – some try to get away with things like that. Many things like these happen in our life. What we should understand is that any advice given is done so for our well being. Unless our faith is solidified in that person or party or wherever the source of the decision-making entity is, we are not going to take whatever is given to us to the best of our capabilities.

If you received advice and acted contrary to it, I would suggest that you do not keep feeling bad all the time because that is not doing you any good. One should learn from the process so that next time, one can do better. If we start worrying about, "Why this happened," and "Why I didn't do this," we are wasting the current moment. Time is ticking away, and time is precious. Each moment is precious and should be used in the best possible manner. The saints have always said that we need to live in the present. Let us not worry about the past or the future. If we have done something in the past that is bothering us, the saints do not want us to be worried about it now, or else this moment will also pass away in worrying about what happened. They want us to make the best of this moment. So I would learn from whatever mistake I have made or whatever advice I could not follow, and try to make it right so that next time I am in that situation, I could better myself.

 Q: What should we do when we are in the Master's physical presence and then return home after receiving a lot of Master's love and attention, but find back home that we are not receptive anymore and do not want to meditate? Is this due to our ego being nourished by the attention of the Master, and, if so, how can we overcome our ego?

Because of the spiritual radiation of the Master, when we are in his physical presence it is easy to focus our attention on the Divine. When we are in his presence, our mind is stilled and we receive radiation through his eyes, which makes it easier to focus on the spiritual way. But when we leave that physical presence and return to our homes, we are in a scenario in which we have to deal with day-to-day activities. In that scene, there are many things to do. We get caught up as we start our day. We want to do this and that and generally leave spirituality towards the end. The day passes and the time is gone. What is happening is that the mind is trying its best to keep us away from being focused on Reality. The mind will try all kinds of wiles to keep us away from the Divine. By elating us, by depressing us, by keeping us focused in one activity or another, the mind is focusing our attention away from God. There are many factors to help us stay focused on God.

Saints in the Sant Mat and other traditions talk about meditating early in the morning. They call it the *amrit vela*, which is between 3 and

6 a.m. Amrit vela means the time when the divine nectar is flowing. It is not that the divine nectar is not flowing at all times. The divine nectar is flowing twenty-four hours a day. Guru Arjan Dev Ji Maharaj said that divine nectar is always flowing. It is also called *brahm mahurat,* which means the time to know God. The reason that the early morning hours have been picked by the saints as a good time to meditate is that those hours were always the quietest time of the day. In the old times there were no buildings, paved roads, electricity, cars running all over the place, or telephones working day and night. People would go to sleep early. When it got dark, people would sleep so they could be up at three in the morning. From three to five, or three to six in the morning was the time before the sun came out. As the sun starts to come out, birds start to chirp and distract people. Between the hours of three to six a.m. was the quietest time of day. Even today, usually, that is the quietest time which makes it easier to still the mind. If meditation was the first thing that people did when they got up, then their spiritual aspect of life would be done before they would start anything else. What happens to most of us is that we wake up with the alarm clock, are late for work, brush our teeth, run to catch the train or the bus to work, and are so caught up in our day-to-day activities that we are not focused on what truly helps us – which is meditation.

I would suggest that when we are away from the physical presence of the Master we need to schedule meditation into our lives. We need to make time for our spiritual practices. That will truly help us because, if the day starts calmly, its effect will be with us all day long.

The saints also talk about attending satsangs. We can not be physically with the Master twenty-four hours a day or all the time, even if we live in the same city or close to where he lives. What is a satsang? A satsang is a time in which our attention is focused on

Truth. This word "satsang" means "to be with Truth." Satsang is when the saints talk about God and Truth. When we go there, we get a re-charging. Our attention goes away from worldly affairs and focuses on God. Much has been spoken about the benefits of being in satsang. Periodically, whether once a week or whichever way it fits into our lifestyles, through attending satsang, there is a recharging of our soul. We receive a boost that helps us to deal with day-to-day activities.

When we receive the attention of the Master when physically with him, it is not that our ego is getting boosted and then getting flattened when we go away. When we get the attention of the Master, it is to help us so that when we are not there, we can benefit from that attention. It is only our mind keeping us away from Reality, and that is why we get distracted.

The mind will always entangle us in the activities of the world. The more we get entangled, the further away we go from God. It is important that whenever we are not in the physical presence to try our best to make sure that the day starts with some spiritual practices. Their effect will help us. When we are with the Master and have benefited, then, when we return home, we should be focused on our remembrances of having been there so that our focus is on God.

Q: Before rising above body-consciousness, how can we know God's will?

God's will is not difficult to know once we have a clear understanding of what life is all about. As we pass through life, there are many decisions that we all make. These are based on our understanding of the situation. Before we rise above physical body-consciousness and experience the Divine, our life is generally lived under the control of Kal or *maya*. Under that control we are kind of dragged into the illusionary world. When we are in that state, we first of all need to pray to God that the right things happen in our own life and that God's will, and not our will, be done. Generally what happens is that we have to decide something. If we are careful about gauging the whole situation and make a decision that will not bring any pain into the lives of others, that will be a right decision for us. Generally, what happens is that as human beings, we make those decisions that we think are good for us. Some people do not care enough to see if the decision they make will bring pain into the lives of others. When we force our way and make a decision under those circumstances, we go contrary to God's will. Even though there are many ups and downs in life, and we go through difficulties because we have to pay for our past karma, God's will is generally that there should be love and harmony in everyone's life.

To understand God's will, the criteria that we should use to see if a decision is correct, or not in God's will, is to see if that decision is going to bring happiness and joy into our lives and the lives of others. We should also determine that there will be no pain or difficulty coming to others from that decision. Generally, once we have established that, the decision that we take would be under God's will.

Seventy-five percent of our life is preordained. We still have twenty-five percent free will. It is in that free will that we sometimes make decisions contrary to God's will. It is important to pray to the Lord to help us make the right decisions and to gain guidance to take steps towards our goal of merging our soul in the Lord. We should use whatever information we have in our own hands to the best of our capabilities so that any decisions we make will bring love and harmony into our lives and also into the lives of others.

Q: How can we come to the Master for the sake of the Master and for the spiritual benefit and not come to him only for material or physical benefit or help with worldly problems?

Many times, we come to the Master when we are in trouble. Many people come because they have a physical problem – the doctors tell them their diseases can not be cured. Some come because they are in a financial crunch. Others come because they have emotional or relationship problems. We come to be helped in those areas which we think are important.

Little do we realize that unless the spirit is healed, our mental or physical state is not going to be healed. Little do we realize that some problems we have to pass through are due to our past karmas and activities that have been associated with our soul through our other existences.

Sant Kirpal Singh Ji Maharaj would recount this interesting anecdote. He would say that suppose you have a Master who is sitting in a room. Then, before you get to his room, you have to pass through several other rooms first. Sitting in the first room is a doctor. In another room through which you must pass before you get to the Master's room is a banker. In the room after the banker is another room with a lawyer sitting there. Sant Kirpal Singh Ji would say that most of the people who come to see the Master want to see a super-doctor who can fix all their physical problems. They have a pain here, or cancer, or a problem that can not be solved. But if they come to the super-doctor, who fixes their physical problem, they do not go any further. They are done, and they go home. Then, suppose some people come to the Master because they have a financial problem. They do not have a physical problem, so they bypass the doctor and reach the room with the super-banker. The banker solves their financial problem, so their problem is solved and they go home. They do not go any further towards the Master's room. Then, some people do not have physical or financial problems, but have legal problems. They find help in the room with the super-lawyer who takes care of all their problems. Maybe we can add someone else in another room who takes care of their emotional needs. If their emotional problems are fixed they do not need to go any further. If people feel, "Well, my problem is solved," they then go away. This is why Sant Kirpal Singh Ji said that if you put the doctor, banker, and lawyer outside the door of the Master to solve people's problems, most of the people would find their problems solved and leave; few would be left who had come to the Master for the sake of the Master and spiritual growth. Sant Darshan Singh Ji often said that people do not come for the Master; they come for these kinds of problems to be solved. Many of us live at that level. We do not go beyond that.

When we come to the Master, we should come for our spiritual rejuvenation. We should come for the connection of our soul with God. The Master acts as a catalyst so that the connection of our soul can be made with the divine Light and Sound of God within. The job of the Master is to connect us with that divinity. The Master is not there to connect us with himself. He is there to connect us with the divine Light and Sound of God.

Generally we can not get to that goal, because we are so caught up with our other problems in life. This brings us to the role of the compassion of the Masters; if some of these problems can be solved, then we are better able to focus on Reality. Little do we realize that because of our karmic load, there are ups and downs in life that we have to go through, whether physical, mental, emotional, or financial. There will be times when we will be elated; there will be times when we will be in the doldrums. But unless our spirit is healed, the purpose of our existence in the human body does not get fulfilled.

It is important to recognize that this human existence has a purpose, that we are all here to grow spiritually, to know the Lord, and to merge back in the Lord. This is not a haphazard existence. Our soul, which has been separated from the Lord for aeons and aeons, has been traveling from one existence to another. Through these various existences, we have created karmic loads, which we need to pay off. Unless all that karmic load is paid off, we are not going to be able to merge back into the Creator. We need to attain the state of purity within so that the karmic load – or these layers of mind, matter, and illusion accumulated over our soul – can be removed and we can glimpse our true self. That is what happens when we come into the presence of a Master.

A perfect Master acts like a perfect washerman who cleanses us so that the grime collected on our souls can be removed. As that dirt, grime, and layers of illusion are removed, we experience the reality of who we really are and the purpose of our existence. We recognize that we are conscious and full of the Light and love of God. A perfect Master helps us go within to recognize who we truly are. When we do so, then we definitely are going to reach our goal in life. When we go to a Master, we should always be focused on the spiritual aspect, because once our spirit is healed, all other things will fall into place. Those other problems are all secondary. If we do not recognize that and are merely caught up in outside activities, we do not advance spiritually any further.

When we go to a Master, we should have in our hearts, minds, and souls the goal to grow spiritually and recognize our true selves. We should go with the desire to find divine love within. We should go to him to be able to connect with the Light and Sound of God, because it is only through that connection that we are able to get back to our original state of purity. It is in that pristine state that we are able to soar into the inner regions.

This is the reason that the great saints have talked about being able to inculcate the ethical virtues of humility, selfless service, non-violence, purity, love for all, truth, and compassion. These are stepping stones to spirituality. These are not the goals. These help us reach a state where we are ready for our spiritual growth. When we

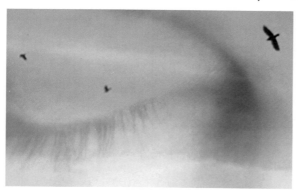

develop ethical qualities, our spiritual growth comes in leaps and bounds.

When we have a spiritual thirst and are searching for Truth, it is helpful to find a spiritual Master. When we do so, it is important that we are receptive when in his presence. Many people in the

West, because they come from an analytical background and are taught since birth to believe only what can be experienced through the five outer senses, have a difficult time on the spiritual path. It is difficult to let their egos go. The whole society is based on self-help, but the spiritual path is one where you need the help of God. It is not a contradiction; it is a question of understanding. Even after doing the most that we can on our own, there are things beyond what we can do. If we do not recognize that, then we will always hit our head against a wall and will not proceed further.

Saints and mystics have said that if we are not receptive and do not come with humility in our hearts, we are not going to benefit. Even if spiritual radiation comes in our direction, if we can not let it sink into us, it will just hit us and bounce off someplace else. For spiritual radiation to sink into us, we need to be receptive. This is the reason that most saints who write poetry describe receptivity as something we can receive from a saint when we are an empty cup. If a cup is already full, nothing can be poured into it. But if we are humble, receptive, pure, loving, and caring, then the divine nectar can definitely pour into every pore of our being, and that is what we need so that we can grow on the spiritual path.

When we are searching for Truth it is important to be open to ideas or experiences beyond the physical, because the spiritual path is way beyond whatever we experience in the physical world. In the physical world we live at the level of our senses. All activities in this physical world are experienced through our senses. We are used to focusing only through our senses of sight, hearing, smell, taste, and touch. Those are the impulses that go into our system and how we react to our physical world. But we can rise above the physical senses and experience the Divine. If we are not open to that, then we will never get there. Only if we are receptive are we going to experience the Divine.

It is similar to what happens to people when there is new technology. Sometimes someone is stuck with the old equipment and does not want to try anything new because they do not know if it will work or not. But once one is open, one finds that some of the new innovations are helpful. One needs to be in an open frame of mind to receive. If we are closed minded and not open to ideas or experiences beyond the physical, then we are definitely not going to gain.

When we are trying to know our true selves, we need to realize that there is more to us than the body and senses. There is more to us than meets the physical eye – there is the spiritual eye between and behind the two eyebrows. That needs to be open. We need to see with that inner eye and hear with our inner ear to experience divinity within. We need to soar on the divine Light and Sound so that our soul can merge back in God. It is not only for the saints and mystics to experience – we all can experience that. We all have been equipped to experience divinity within. It is a question of being able to focus our attention within through accurate meditation. This is why saints and mystics say that when we want to grow spiritually, we need guidance and help, just as we do in any other area in this world. If we come to a Master for guidance with humility and receptivity in our hearts, our spiritual thirst can be fulfilled.

About the Author

Rajinder Singh is one of the world's leading experts in meditation. He is head of Science of Spirituality, a non-profit, non-denominational organization with centers in forty countries, which provides a forum for people to learn meditation, experience personal transformation, and bring about inner and outer peace and human unity. He has presented his powerful, yet simple technique to millions of people throughout the world through seminars, meditation retreats, television and radio shows, magazines, and books. His method of achieving inner and outer peace through meditation has been recognized and highly respected by civic, religious, and spiritual leaders wherever he goes.

His books and publications, translated into over fifty languages, include *Empowering Your Soul through Meditation,* and *Inner and Outer Peace through Meditation,* published by HarperCollins Thorsons Element, with a foreword by H.H. the Dalai Lama, *Visions of Spiritual Unity and Peace, Ecology of the Soul, Education for a Peaceful World,* and in Hindi, *Spirituality in Modern Times,* and *True Happiness,* audiotapes, videotapes, and hundreds of articles which have been published in magazines, newspapers, and journals throughout the world. His programs are broadcast throughout the world on television, radio, and over the Internet.

Rajinder Singh

He is head of the Human Unity Conference and was President of the 7th World Religions Conference. He was a major presenter of the 1993 Parliament of World Religions held in Chicago, and at the World Conference on Religions and Peace held in Rome in 1994. He has convened major world conferences for peace and unity such as the 16th, 17th, 18th, 19th, and 20th International Human Unity Conference and annual conferences on Human Integration and on Global Mysticism.

Rajinder Singh has been honored with numerous awards and tributes, including a Peace Award given in June 1997 by the Interfaith Center of New York and the Temple of Understanding at a ceremony attended by United Nations NGOs (Non-government Agencies). A day was even named after him in Baltimore as Rajinder Singh Day. He led a meditation for thousands of people at the 50th Anniversary of the United Nations held in New York, a prayer at a ceremony to honor the United Nations Secretary General, and was a special invitee to the National Prayer Breakfast in February 1997 over which the president presided. He addressed the United States Coast Guard Academy on the topic of the moral dimensions of leadership. He also spoke at the opening session of the United Nations Millennium Peace Summit for Religious and Spiritual Leaders in 2000 in the General Assembly. He received a Distinguished Leadership Award from I.I.T. (Illinois Institute of Technology) for his work in the fields of peace and spirituality. In South America, he received honorary doctorates from two universities for his contribution to peace, education, and spirituality.

Rajinder Singh is active in helping humanity. His organization is involved in social service activities such as free allopathic, homeopathic, and ayurvedic clinics and free eye camps. It has provided assistance to people who underwent natural disasters such as the volcano in Colombia, the earthquake in Mexico, floods in Delhi, and the hurricane in Florida, and has rebuilt one of the cities devastated by the earthquake in Gujarat, including building homes, a school, and a meditation/community center.

His background has been in science. He received his B. Tech degree from I.I.T. (Indian Institute of Technology), in Madras, India, and a M.S. degree from I.I.T. (Illinois Institute of Technology), Chicago, Illinois. He had a successful twenty-year career in computers and communications and worked in Research and Development areas. His work in the field of science, computers, and communication has given him the ability to have a scientific approach to spirituality. He makes the science of spirituality and the practice of meditation easy for people around the world to understand and practice for themselves.